The Heart

―――――――――――――――――――

Hector Agustin

Table of Contents

Preface..9

Introduction 16

In the Beginning..35

A World of Idols...69

Persuasion and Deception (*A World of Idols: Part 2*)...............89

Susceptibilities of the
Heart..124

The Sculpture..140

Who God Could Be...141

Ode to the Essence...166

Fleeting Meditations..170

"So long as the infantile ego consciousness is weak and feels the strain of its own existence as heavy and oppressive...it has not yet discovered its own reality and differentness."

- Erich Neumann, The Origins and History
of Consciousness

I carry You in my memory, my cells, and most of all, my Heart.
I couldn't erase You even if I tried.

Preface

    My mother talked about getting a house cat for a long time. It had already been five years since we began feeding stray cats, seeing generations go as they came by. This June saw a particular bunch of kittens fall under my mother's protection. She cornered them near the entrance of our home. With a wooden plank, she made them a 'wall', providing them shelter from the neighborhood dogs. These dogs could be quite vicious and we had already lost one to the jaws of a pitbull. It was a tragic scene. My mom witnessed it all. We didn't live in the most affluent of neighborhoods, so guard dogs, without a leash often, were the kind that roamed around. From this particular bunch we could tell which cat was the prettiest. He had blue eyes and he was beige. He had very blue eyes. He was covered with a coat softer than a baby's gaze. We knew he was *the one.* I thought he was cute. My mother started calling him a name that she used for every cat so Viviano was the name, his government name, at least, but we would call him 'BB'. He had a personality and a way about him as most cats do. I would make fun of his meow. It was never as harsh or authoritative as his personality was. I liked the cat. I did.

    One day, a rare storm came over my hometown of

Laredo in South Texas. Storms are something of a miracle down there. They still are. I worried that our feline friends wouldn't fare well under those conditions. I'm talking heavy winds, pouring rain, pairs of lightning per second. The other kittens in the bunch had all taken shelter with their mother. BB did not receive the same affection. She largely excluded him from the protection she offered her other young. Perhaps the mother felt our affinity for him or smelled it on him or something. We handled him so often. Nevertheless, I felt something should occur to prevent any harm to this kid. I remember the rain was cold, the wind even colder. I remember the neighbor's palm trees losing branches and I stared with wide eyes and stiff lip at the leaves falling from the heights above the electrical lines. Our garbage can was at the neighbor's house. Something had to be done, I thought.

    I went outside and made a small shelter for him. I'd cup him in my hand and place him in the carved out box. He'd walk right out of it, back into the rain. 'Cats aren't meant to like rain', I thought. And so, I would go back and forth, putting him back in the dry fortress I had made and there he would go boldly again running back to the danger, straight back into the rain. I eventually went inside and expressed my concerns to my mother who suggested I use the cage we had in storage. It seemed like a good enough idea. I went inside and headed to the garage to look for it. Eventually, I was able to pull enough boxes away to take out the cage. I prompted it near the front door, inside, and went out into the storm to look for the boy. Took me a while to do so but eventually I found him, huddled in a corner (not the one I made for him), shivering and crying. I grabbed him with a scoop and he immediately started yelping. I couldn't blame the cat, this giant scooped him up from his environment to a point higher than he had ever felt comfortable climbing to. I held him at my chest and brought him inside. Little guy must've felt like he was mountain climbing. I opened the cage and set him there. A towel and a water bowl were next to him. He was alright.

Oh, how he cried. He cried and he cried. I sat near him and waited for something to happen, but he just kept crying. I wasn't confused about why he was crying. Regardless, I tried to think about what he could be thinking, if he could at all. His brain is probably the size of a peanut, I thought. I deduced if he could think, if it could be put into words, translated into a language with meanings something along the lines of ours, it'd probably be a scream something along the lines of 'leave' or 'get me out of here'. Even then, his little brain surely lacked the capacity to meet these words at their pronunciation. Obviously, right? But his instinct surely drew out the movements carrying the spirit of them. Despite his 'suffering', I was not moved to move him back to the outside he was accustomed to as I knew the danger that awaited him out there.

I understood why he was here with me, away from his family. I empathized with him. I did but ultimately permitted his discomfort to continue. I knew the future awaiting him, the endless treats he was in line to lose. I was sympathetic. He was only a kitten, young and lost. Thing is, his safety and air-conditioned future were in jeopardy. My boy's kingdom awaited. We had lost strays to storms before. I was not moved by his yelps as a result. As I sat there next to him, I got to thinking. I put together that his little brain could not understand that this night was his salvation, the beginning of the rest of his life, that it distinguished him from his brothers and sisters. I was also not blind to the fact he would never realize this, too. As I sat longer, I could not help but think of myself. I thought of all the times I ever cried. I recalled all the times I felt bad about anything, any time I cried myself to sleep about an issue. I recalled all of the situations I ever evaluated where I named the conditions in a way that fooled myself into believing were unjust or unfair.

I compared myself to this cat and was humbled to imagine that my brain and perception were not the biggest things in this world. I thought of brain power and concluded I did not have much. I could and would not know everything. So I began to think about all of the things my little brain could not fit. I recalled how many issues of the past saw their way through. Seeing the way everything sort of blended itself into everything, rarely did an issue not get resolved, I thought. I began to contemplate if I was ever "protected", if I, like this 'kidnapped' cat, was ever "rescued". The cat stopped crying the moment he felt his known ground the next morning. But by this time, the storm had passed and he returned well-fed. He cried through the night and survived a storm one of his brothers did not. He was not crying when he was eating, though. It was a cage he was in, for sure. However, it was a cage with a very protective purpose, albeit he couldn't see that. I couldn't help but imagine my own "cages", if I've ever been 'saved' before, of all of the sights that escape my perception simply because they were out of my comfort zone.

In time, after a few traumatizing veterinarian visits and more 'hard times' for Viviano, he went on to become our first housecat. I fell in love with this cat. In his tenure as his senior regency of South Laredo, the official title in his headquarters, also known as my home, much occurred in my life and the lives of those around me. This is how tenures of those in power go. He never lost his 'ghetto' mentality and grassroots soul, as demonstrated by his ability to socialize, fist fight, and detect cockroaches. He never came around to trusting us very much, even after all the toys and food. He liked things a certain way but he never rejected a stranger. He did learn to demand things from us and reject us simultaneously. He grew alongside us, inspiring smiles that would likely not have happened had he not been there. The arguments would not be interrupted by his very high-pitched meow with his absence. It was incredibly difficult to remain hostile when Viviano would prop himself up on a chair and begin yelling with us. He had a knack to do this when we were all arguing. It was great. He is remembered as a fair leader to this day. My mother who smiled once a month found herself smiling once a week and eventually once a day. That same year, my father suffered a heart attack. He had grown tough and bitter by the everyday toil of working-class demands. He was never a cat person, either. The man that would initially complain of the cat's hair, meowing, and running around would, after a brush with death, be the one who cried most when Viviano died one Friday morning about two years after this story began. His Excellency departed us one for the Kingdom of eternal treats and clean litter. My prayers went unanswered I thought, but then I remembered how me and this little guy got started.

    I was bereaved by the death of this animal. I prayed to a god that he would see it through. I loved that. I worried that my sensitive mother would not suffer another heartbreak. It tore me to imagine a long life ahead without the privilege of hearing, seeing, or touching the sweet boy. I still have the craving to do so, a heaven where I could do so is a nice thought. He was never the friendliest nor the most affectionate, so it helps to know my love for him was not contingent on what I recieved, on the fact of my person being loved. He often looked at us as if he owned the land we walked on and we simply had the pleasure of accompanying him on it. I went through a great deal of more loss after this. It was far from the only tragedy to beset us, but it was a unique one for me. The boy could not speak, nor think, nor write. Yet, he impacted my father and mother in ways that left them two different individuals than before they made this feline friend of ours. They smiled with him more than me!

What impacted me about the experience was the person I was after it all. Meeting and tending to the cat taught me a lot. It broadened the horizons of my consciousness. His death made me stronger as a thinker and a person. He was a product of life and the great chain of history. Then again, so are we. Many cats had to be born for this specific cat to come about. He was a friend in and of Being, a product of the natural world. We shared the fact that we are animals with our own slices of consciousness. In our case, we are particularly moral animals, doing what we think or feel is right. The key here is *what we think or feel* is right. What he thought was right was often a smack or a chomp to get his point across. What felt right for me was based on an urge to protect him during that storm that one night. Instinct guided us both. The animal brought out the best in us, providing an opportunity for us to reimagine compassion, care, and empathy. He made us more in-tuned with life around us by his way of understanding that or this. Ultimately, he made us appreciate one another a little more. We didn't think he would pass away. I really didn't believe his slice of consciousness would slip from this plane so soon. I thought I was going to have him around for many years. What would have been just another stray cat destined for an arduous and cyclical life of braving the elements and relieving hunger became the spark and glue of a household. He held his position nobly, giving back to those who served him most loyally.

He sparked a chain in my thinking that led me to do this, albeit many moons later. We do not know enough. That awakened a lot in me. For me, that fact started with him. It led me to a profound interest and affinity for practices and principles most people do not talk about very openly. But despite the fact we don't talk about the glaring interconnectivity of all things and the relevance of those practices and principles, we all feel them and often secretly agree to them. We live with a constant ignorance of information and knowledge. And even when we get a 'grip' on something, the dynamics of it change so often that by the time we know it, we lose it. But perhaps instead of making life harder by avoiding it or making our understanding rigid, we can embrace it. The knowledge learned after the concession of permanent ignorance may just hold the key to our salvation, the key to permanent flexibility and stability simultaneously. We should see there is nothing weak or disadvantageous in admitting we could know more, nothing embarrassing about the fact that we don't know enough. Our little brains can only understand so much and we have the world and our livelihoods to lose when we believe or act like we 'know'. Beautifully enough, we have the world to gain when we admit we do not.

    If we run through life, we will miss many things we would have caught if we had only walked. In this life, we will miss many "BB's" as we walk the streets. Our feet have been confined to very limited parts of the world. We get worked up so effortlessly by cages not to our liking, rejecting free and open pastures in favor of prisons of our own liking. We can become unimaginably challenged to let go of all we know by the Heart's invitation to go to those lands that were meant for us. Much of this is a journey, but most of us just know that as life. We don't even know what we don't know. *No matter the fear and trembling the ignorance may inspire, the key to salvation may be hidden in our endurance and attitude in it.* A cat's cry inspired a thought that activated a new way of living. Who knows all the glory and knowledge this tiny brain won't ever get to touch or comprehend? A cat inspired that thought for me.

Introduction

Not much is in our control. In fact, nearly everything we see, touch, and interact with is fundamentally out of our hands. Much of this composition is going to be dedicated to how people deal with that fact. Despite it being based on my experience, mine is a human experience. For that reason, I believe it is in large part an experience we can share and relate to each other about. Like any other, I went through situations and found myself in contexts that forced me to sit down, quell my delusions, as to to see exactly what is going on inside that has brought me here to be needing to regroup. What's the fuss inside all about? For example, we begin with wanting something and then we may chase after it to 'get it', but I observed that chasing it would often result in more demands. Doing an action didn't yield a result, it often incurred the need for something else so as to arrive at a separate opportunity to get what I was aiming at. Doing was not as simple as I thought. The point is suddenly not as simple as the fleeting but attractive desire I started with. Then, often by our hand, we exponentiate our lack of control in a situation or totally restructure it with a definitive move all because we chased after one desire.

Nothing can be undone, too. That's pretty unfortunate. And alive as we are, being the fairly intelligent primates we are lucky enough to be, we are dealt a unique hand. We are forced to deal with natural forces that drive us, the kind that breaks our concentration and entices others to act on us and us on them. Additionally, we have to deal with the awareness of that. And with those same forces, we are challenged to drive ourselves in and out of the trouble we get ourselves into as far as we percieve. It seems like a neat game, consciousness and what not, but experiencing it can be extremely disorienting, confusing, and complicated. Enduring and unraveling it can be extremely difficult. It's the reason we say life is hard. Most of these forces are older than time. Ambition and our primitive roots form the impulses that demonstrate these forces. They start somewhere profound and reach the superficial level of existence as our desires. They are of natural origin and they take us to the places and practices we thought we would never get to, ones we never thought possible. If not most, all. For instance, these forces have led us to produce concrete and abstract structures. Some of these include grandiose pieces of architecture, intricate states and governments, and a countless number of savvy tools and practices.

Despite the age-old forces in us, the time we live in is one quite like no other. The 'twenty-first century' has brought us broad new abilities not afforded to any century before ours. Technology has prompted leaps in our capacities before, but our time is different. We live in a time that routinely breaks limitations we've known for millions of years. We can do things in this age we've thought impossible for dozens of thousands of years. We can go to places once thought inaccessible and get to those places faster than ever before. We can duplicate things at rates never before seen, instantaneously almost. We can move through the air. We can restart hearts. We can collect and enjoy bread en masse without farming anything ourselves. We can talk to people in other countries, the ones that are on the other side of the ocean. Engines are a thing. We can do business with people dozens of thousands of miles away, all without seeing their face. This generation gets to consume in unfathomable quantities and don't even get me started with the internet. From globalization, to airplanes, to the internet, to video calls, and the resultant atmosphere we experience as popular culture, what a truly unique time to be in where so many livelihoods are as connected as ours.

    This new interconnectivity carries immense implications for you and me. It seems, however, many amongst this generation carry the foolish notion that because of these new luxuries that we have transcended the primitive forces of "the past". I argue we have not. I refuse to accept that because many get to enjoy the commodities included in corporately prepared condominiums that we are somehow removed from our savagery. Instead, I argue that because of our unlimited supply of 'governmentally treated' chemically-processed water, entertainment, and fast food, we are just blind to it. Advertisement doubles down on retaining a uniformity among the meanings the masses impose one another. They would prefer we think of the same things, usually their products or symbols, so they could sell that idea and prevent any slippage in terms of its relevance. The young believe they do things 'for themselves'. See, we are so far from our relationship with Nature that many see animals and assume their nature is one far from ours. Looking beyond differences, as we will find with most people, their nature is made to reach the same ends. Many of the statesmen and the politicians believe their plans do not border on classical tribalism. We glorify the consumption of flesh because of a few seasonings and spices. We think our meanings and interpretations are what a social group is all about. We think our symbols are special, confusing the ends we use them for with the social aesthetic they provide for the interpretation of our surface. And the truth is that they are all structured to acquire these eerily similar ends, sex and survival mainly.

We distort reality to create this 'reason' for thinking the way we do. We drape our rationale with this blanket of 'righteousness', but often this 'righteousness' is nothing more than an evaluative lens we use to assess how effectively something reinforces our rights or access to our needs. We may believe we have superseded our savagery, and for the sake of our comfort, outsource evil's existence to "those people" or "their kind", to the Other. The truth is, however, nobody is very much removed from our savagery. Not even close. While we don't have to activate much of our hunting abilities when ordering fast food or grocery shopping, or so it would appear, our bodies do carry the history of our evolution. The chance to eat meat and pick fruit and vegetables freely was once an effort that did require much more of those 'primal' instincts. But let me be the one to tell you, give someone the right conditions and the corresponding needs, you'll see that primitivity kick off and overtake that someone very quickly. These instincts now sit atop the controls for the nuclear bombs, weapons of mass destruction. They sit deluded and arroagantly in thecomforts offered by the West's affluence. They drive and dominate the maintenance of the totalitarian states. The primal tribalism of the genocides of years ago may be believed to reside in the atrocities of the history books or the wilderness of the jungle. Any look at the world today stands to prove this a delusional belief.

We can be greatly comforted (and resultantly grow egregiously delusional and self-absorbed) with the capacities and implications of our new commercial privileges. The interconnectivity and consolidated globalization in culture and trade have done this much for us. We make schedules to meet the demands of the social world. We engineer our aspirations to fit its molds and shape our interactions and conversations to remain enjoyable to the folks in them. We evaluate actions on the basis of success and failure, of good and evil. One thing they have not done, however, is reform the patterns our attention gets shaped and we consistently fail to reshape the directional tendencies our movements take. We have not captured the essence of the Person, but we're trying to. You know. After the ambitions of youth pass, one often finds a person, nor a principle, not even a lover satisfies. No institution can make the person. No amount of prestige can do this for us. Wholeness comes from someplace within. Our societies have yet to capture the wholeness of a human personality. Despite the tweaks and detailing we sweat over to 'perfect' our systems, we still have people and situations that go another way. Criminality, betrayal, and disrespect have not eradicated themselves. The wind that makes these is a result of this comfort, this arrogance, this newly found ubiquitous delusion.

And as a result of this failure, problems exist that are unique to our time. Some are old, some are new, some are old and have come in a new way. This time's inhabitants seem to be entranced by objects and conceptions that challenge their instincts, especially ones that test their body's capacity. We seem to be enamored with the ones that take us over. These are often the practices and products that tend to break us apart. I would be one of these people. We can grow infatuated with and addicted to machinations of our imaginations, the kind that lead to fascinations that force our instincts to work against our better nature. As a result, our behavior can compromise our values by the truth that we are not exactly who we say we are. With these tools, whether they're for currency, recreation, or occupation,

an overriding of our natural safeguards can occur by virtue of
our instinct's demands for pleasure. Some bask in their
egotistical sense through social media, often to the extent one's
self esteem may grow dependent, insensitive, or blind to others.
They can give themselves to these practices, even deadly ones.
In glorifying these images, we may want to become one of these,
especially when that image is the 'norm' for a social group. A
betrayal of the self occurs, however, when we go along with the
pursuit of images that go against our values or how we feel
things ought to be. I think a lot of what occurs today enables
this kind of betrayal.

In the aim to bask in that image, we may destroy much,
even our value structure, compromising our capacity to love.
Because we can form neural pathways that leave us preoccupied
and fascinated with dangerous habits and propositions,
decisions that go against the way we think things ought to be
leave us more damaged than before we decided to see what all
the fuss was about. Every time the Heart says no, but the
actions scream yes, great harm to the reputation, to other's
knowledge and our person's dignity occurs. Often, this is in the
nothingness and vanity that fuels the chase of our egocentric
endeavors. Many in our time don't, refuse to, or never learn to
consider the Self 'outside' of the ideas that come and go in our
minds. Many of us go on 'making' our personalities, not out of a
primitive foundation or the lessons of this life, but the vanities
our societies encourage. And often, without a clue, we fail to see
how powerless, careless, inconsiderate, lazy, and rude we
actually are. We take comfort in the prestige, the fleeting, the
vain.

But this is not to say humans are inherently evil, only
that we can be extremely oblivious, painfully unaware, of the
implications our actions carry. As a result, we can act with
insensitivity for long periods of time and not realize it until after

numerous periods of long periods of time. At times, we arrive at the total neglect of our values out of the simple fact others would appreciate the abandonment of those values. This is how we come to the degradation of our person and the widespread breakdown of morality. Consequently, the family, too. Our intuitions end up neglected, as does our internal morality in favor of the convenience our obedience to the larger crowd offers us. All of this comes to fruition because of the fact we frequently refuse to stop for a moment to look both ways before we cross our mental street. That intersection is sense and nonsense, of course. In the cases where we do harm others and ourselves, we come to the crossroads of our inner persons.

Our minds will show us signs, too. Whether through nightmares or anxiety or self-destructive activity, all these demonstrate difficulty or even the inability to tolerate what is within. The external attempt to resolve reflects our avoidance of conditions that our person would not be happy to be associated with. These things we are not willing to tolerate, grow in our psyche and person as tension in regards to mental objects. The avoidance comes to represent itself in all the ways we categorize something as 'wrong'. This 'wrong' grows often, if not always, with adjacent respect to what we felt was 'right' for the moment. Sometimes we see harms occur and actually feel our perception's relevant wisdom scream out to us with warnings about an act's implications for us and still do not find the courage to change. We'll do it or ignore it anyway. We strangely do this very often. What feels good and right and appropriate can come to feel wrong, too. In the confusion, we may try to get away from these reminders. But with the immense mass of information we juggle when deciding, thinking, and introspecting, can we really blame ourselves for enjoying relief or losing track of our attention? I think not. Should we be careful with regards to this inattention? I think so.

We have so many opportunities to get distracted with each distraction pulling us each to a unique end. Other people can be our distractions, so can our habits. We are guided by and to opinions, options, and occasions. We inherit many of these desires, too. And society can grow to encompass these desires and develop them into expectations the old steer the young towards. They are all ingrained into our biological, social, and psychological tendencies. They are all advocated for under the guise of their 'use'. They lead us to lead a life that resembles a battle to control our impulse for the new, leading us to compartmentalize our difference, to make peace where the old and new can't reconciliate. We redefine the truth. Our goals become tunnels to get through, and with the old wisdom, transform into rubrics for the everyday to get our goals through. This is all good, more or less. Sometimes for harsher, sometimes for better, sometimes to death. The Mind has inherited molds for objects it has become historically acquainted with. Independently of education, the Mind, too, inherits a genetic code that helps us map some of the world's symbolic architecture.

For example, we rationalize the experience of interacting with people as examples, lessons, and teachers or all of the above. Sometimes, all at the same time. We can be carriers of this or that, funnels of the images others have painted on us. We can be messengers, saviors, and pains in the ass. Equally, we can be facilitators and disruptors. We can be examples of both what is better and what is worse. And in such a relative age, I think our interpretation of things, events, and people leads to the majority of the trouble we get into. Someone's right is another's wrong and when we get together to reach a right, we struggle to agree on that right. So I see these words as greatly scrutinized in today's age as demonstrated by the fight to prove what is right to this person or that group. The thing we don't seem to have a problem with the existence of that 'right', just the place of where the red line lies. And even though we live in a time that is remarkably relative in many respects, I still believe there are better situations and worse ones. I think anyone with experience knows that, too. The way things come about in our lives is going to be largely owed to the usage of our abilities in the light of our designated circumstances. The challenge of our lives will be to wiggle our way through what we were born into and wiggling our way out of the trouble we've gotten ourselves into. For this reason, we are challenged to learn about ourselves. We are asked to learn about and from others, too. Others will learn to do the same while learning what needs to be done and said under the premise of improving human society, of a flourishment whose bounties will be reaped by me and you and our kids and kids' kids, too. Our responses to what is outside of our control and the amount of attention we give to things that are will determine what we leave behind and gain in this world. It will also determine what direction the future will head to. The temperament of one's perception going into anything will determine the capacity of a person's response with respect to every opportunity and every issue. Like any system, we release outputs out of the way we handle inputs, the same goes for food.

    We possess many abilities as humans, from intuition to creativity. When we conjure up great images in our head, or visions of our desires, we can do some pretty great things with them. We have achieved empires and livelihoods out of them. We have also made a mockery, disaster, traps, chains of deception, including mass murder out of them. Despite the union we share with them as beings of Nature, when we hear of these things, we turn away, mince, scowl, or revolt at them, many act as though the sources of these acts were something separate from us. The reality is they occurred out of a spirit like ours, a human one. We make these things happen out of the chain of our intention, we rarely imagine how far we can go. That is until we do, then we can't imagine how even further, all the while hating to be reminded of how far we've forced ourselves to go. This is the cycle that leads to self hatred. But even our worst mistakes, my friends, are bound to the same naturalism that made us, the one inspiring us and sustaining us. And while we have tools like never before at the palm of our hand, I don't think for a moment they take us out of our natural cage. A friend of mine called it a flesh prison. A tool that can give us information about somewhere else cannot put us there. Eyes on another's highlights don't give the sensation of being there. We don't know what is going on inside our neighbors, we can only relate. That, my friends, takes conscious and careful effort. It takes care. So I think that if we have worked to achieve privileges like the ones previously mentioned, but still possess the same savage spirit, we ought to be careful to keep an order that is 'humane', civil, respectful, decent moving forward.

    The stirrings of our Hearts show the languages of the sciences at play. These stirrings established world religions. I see no divorce between them. Our Hearts spur romance, treachery, but they also maintain Fortune 500 companies. They inspire some to act in a way that leads them to endure lifetime sentences in prison. It inspires others to sentence them to life. As vessels of potential and change, I believe we are 'entrusted' by nature to carry out its game. A course of action I think worthy of entertaining revolves around the idea of how we are managing our time. I think it ought to promote a vision us and others can agree is desirable to see. Relating experiences in our histories can offer insights into what helps you win, grow. We can do 'good' if we want to. The other option is we don't. In all the things that could be, there exists potential and in all change that does occur, we can see the universe dancing before our very eyes. And for those of us who prefer to see growth over decay, improvement over destruction, love over hate, I think a mass effort in our lives is what leads us to becoming just that. It is really something to see just how harmful we can become. I experienced that myself. I think if we intend to make the world a little less hateful, politics a little less deceitful, and our relationships just a little less spiteful, that we must make this choice to be and do good.

Like computers, we are wired to be a certain way under certain conditions under certain circumstances. So, though we may 'choose' to do good, we may be acting according to our internal conditioning. So when I speak of doing 'good', I must make a damn good case for what 'good' is, why it is even relevant, and make it good enough to go against the vast "emptiness" of the universe. Nihilism has grown rampant and the idea that 'we are simply floating monkeys on a rock' has achieved widespread popularity. We may be doing what the natural law has etched into our nerves. It's a hell of an argument, I'll admit. With war, dead children, famine, and many more tragedies, I have to go against what seems to be a total indifference from the universe. But this 'indifference' is simply how it seems to us. We swallow it like a tough pill. We recommend others to swallow it too, consistently defining maturity by our ability to swallow it again and again. When nature's demands destroy us and our dreams, we often sigh with distress and deem it wisely as 'it is what it is'. We extend a variation of the same advice to others when we see their dreams fade into unwanted change. We urge each other not to go against the instinct nature has etched into us.

But why? The truth is we are a part of Nature and even Nature has a nature. That nature is what rules the direction Nature will take. It imposes over all and caves for none. We get hungry when we lack food. We experience arousal. And while we may not want to have a feeling or cause trouble, we will be called to bring that trouble and it's resultant trouble forth. We must accept the nature of our relation with Nature. Limits are limits, force is force, and what will cause change will do so whether we personally agree with it or not. Nature, this way, could be seen as the greatest governing body reigning over us in this universe. If it says death must be, then that is what will be. Dealing with knowledge comprises a great portion of the pain. We may see it all as cold, empty, void of human warmth. And while I see our times question the worth of rules, I see they still very much achieve their regulatory aim. We can't escape them. Therefore, I think if we want to do anything worthwhile in this life, we have to learn the patterns. We have to come to understand them in others and more importantly, ourselves. Maybe then, we can face the indifference of this universe with an attitude that does not exponentiate her pain. Only with this understanding of self can we assure ourselves the world is not on track to find itself blowing herself to shreds or full of lost sinners. We will decide whether our children can smile, grow to experience love, and make lives better than the ones we did, ones where they won't lose.

    No human sat down and decided these natural rules. They rule regardless, moving our groups and persons much like a government. Just like our human governments, Nature is organized, displaying a tendency and affinity for unspoken hierarchy. While a socially constructed government may fail to enforce its rule, with the lawbreaker evading punishment, Nature never fails to recall its debt when the time comes. We have to deal with punishment and promotion in this life. Some of these punishments are periodical, some are lifetime sentences, and some even result in death. Nature's laws don't punish us like our judicial systems do, but it does impose. We cannot survive under certain conditions. We can be physically destroyed. But we can also be mentally affected, as well. The psyche is the other side of this human life. Just as some actions weaken our body, some actions weaken the mind. And oftentimes, these changes are predictable. Other times, Nature decides. The key is to prepare for what we can, procuring strength for the times one will not.

We can behave in a way that undermines, reduces, or even erases our bargaining power, our willpower. The psyche may lose its potency, its incentive to explore. We may even fall in love with the behaviors that do this to us. We can self harm and worse, even self destruct. The acts may become part of our lives and we may even come to hate ourselves for those sets of behaviors. We may be aware of why we do them, but not about the reasons we choose not to stop. And if we do not know why we do them or why we won't stop, we never really pause to see or stop a behavior's cyclical manifestation in our lives. This way, the politicians can roar about change here or there, addicts can claim they'll stop when they want to but if the fundamentals rely on a certain prize earned in a certain action or habit, they won't. So it goes, my friends, without an understanding of our inner nature, the internal will determine the exterior and work us. All the while, we may come to spend our lives merely catching up to the consequences. We can live never acting, only reacting. Among those reactions, we will likely resort to that inner nature to address these consequences. However, we will likely come to simply reinforce the habit, leading us to do it all over again.

Life, my friends, does not have to be confined to its consequences or our habitual misbehaviors. *We have the ability to change, recover, and get better.* A failure to accept change always results in pain and loss. Yet, despite all the pain our addictions, narcissism, and gluttony cause, our time seems to be firmly committed to testing the limits of these ethical boundaries. Our time constantly contradicts itself. I am a part of our time. But most of the time, as we do what we said we would not, we do not necessarily feel it is the wrong thing. Our mind may recall the general moral evaluation society offers for a practice or phenomenon. Their opinion may be helicoptering our actions in our minds and our rebellion is our attempts at freedom from it. Regardless, the Heart does as it sees fit. Amazingly, however, this call, this itch to do what is right is in place by our consciousness. Nature gave us consciousness. She calls out to us to do what she wants us to see in herself. The paradox is that we exist in a state that is part of nature, carries its motion and code, yet is bound by a state of particularity that conflicts with the rest of Nature around us. This way we are simultaneously driven by nature while our emotions make us feel far from it. When we move far away enough from the recognizable conditions conducive to Nature's proliferation, we tend to call it a disorder. In short, we think it's wrong when it doesn't work. So Nature will give us the feeling of comfort and pleasure, but simultaneously put us in a spot where that comfort and pleasure can be the opposite of the direction of our intentions or goals. Then, the hard part is deciding what direction is best when deciding what we know is wrong. And our Minds will try, they'll trick our will often. And if at times we cannot trust our own minds to stop its nonsense, how are we supposed to know which way to go? That, my friends, is the fun part. I love the excitement.

      We have built systems, governments and law books based on providing that guidance to our interior compass. Everyone is guided to what they find 'righteous' in the moment. And when I use the word righteous, I do not mean moral. Society has its understanding of what is right, which is what serves to proliferate it. Much of what is right is understood under this growth-hungry light. Our morals are not reflective of what Nature would prefer. Many argue with God because of this. Cancer comes, children go, accidents happen. People are at the crossroads of this dissonance between Nature and righteousness. Even if it manifests as a person choosing to or not to act, or coming to realize a choice was one of foolishness or nobility. I think we ought to grow up and realize people don't always act out of a moral determination, but more often the one they perceive will satisfy their natural demands. Thus, we can come to see how some people can be so helpful and others so harmful. Everyone has a different picture of what they need and want and those wants and needs contradict each other the whole way through. They contradict ours. So we can imagine all the disagreements and conflicts that can arise simply because people are so unique in their needs and how they choose to meet them. Most of our habits demonstrate this paradoxical conundrum.

Furthering this natural 'righteousness', however, I notice that many of our conceptions of 'right' have some connection to the goals of the natural law. Most humans would appreciate the idea of feeding their loved ones. We seek health for those we love, ideally for ourselves. Yet, despite people commending health and recommending it, they often reject the better nature of getting it. Some can even get so far from it as to declare no 'better' exists at all. Some may convince themselves there is no purpose to advance a 'better'. I say this is a great mistake, a tragic one. Today, the challenge of our new understanding can lead us to grow skeptical of the abstract aspects of our existence. We can fall victim to scientism, an adoration of our scientific process or a reliance on our analytical habit. Life, however, is nothing to be on the attack with. We need not guide our lives by what we do not know, we can live with the excitement of it. What we do not know is nothing to be afraid of. Believing it is something worth fearing leaves out the entirety of the universe unknown. What fear prevents us from living results in life that does not get to be lived. To live large we are called to have a little bit of faith. And as long as we lack it, we are likely to negate the 'better' today and tomorrow. However, someone who has experienced loss, pain, hardship, hunger, homelessness, or worse, brought it on others is likely to reject any nihilistic disposition of this sort.

    People might continue to do things they do not like, acts that harm others, not because they like them, but because they refuse to see the act's vanity, its harms to one's self worth. When no one tells us what is right and wrong, we can go down dangerous, deteriorative, and damning paths unknowingly. If we do not believe we are worthy of better, I wish you good luck in finding the will to choose it. With so many distractions, with so many opinions, and the force of our loved one's words, we can come to be convinced we are not worthy. Others can do this to a person. One person can produce a great deal of damage. Those dirty habits can extend out to others and love for that person can introduce them to another. Others can get contaminated, styled and learned, by the acts we take to avoid 'them'. This can happen to an entire nation. The deceived become resentful and maliciousness can take over. As truth becomes increasingly relative and the reluctance to share it remains, we can grow skeptical as a society, as a nation, as a person. In that doubt, we inevitably disconnect.

    In the disconnection, a sort of tunnel vision can overtake one's perception. The disconnected and dissociated person can structure their life to accommodate for the places, people, or purposes that give them any sense of connection. The human may develop disturbing habits intended to soothe their internal turmoil. While others can see it clearly, the one enduring the cycle of them may not. The Other gets disregarded and the will becomes one other it. Some get taught that no one deserves what others have. Some aren't taught to mitigate the feeling with self-respect. We can also get taught that others do not deserve what we have. When we believe our desires and reality are equal or work in tandem for each other we can grow in a disturbing manner. The Self and Other conception gets disordered. A disturbed psyche yields disturbing behavior. We can come to take what another has earned. We steal. As one wrongs another, love can disappear if the hate gets the chance to grow in that love's way. By this point, culture scrambles to return to order and the one that comes out tends to be a disordered one. And in that conflict, my friends, is where we begin to lose our sense of identity, our society's purpose, and ultimately, our incentive to be moral, our friends.

    We can come to hate ourselves because of what we have done. We can come to hate others and hate the parts in ourselves that make us act in the manners that reflect that hatred. In this state of self-loathing, things unravel into chases for relief, deception gets implemented to cover one's tracks, and self-contradiction grows as 'better' judges their personal reality. The ideals in one become blurry. We can grow dastardly confused. We may curse the 'better' because we believe it is unattainable. We get resentful. We may do so because we believe we are not worthy of that better and through projection deem the world incapable of realizing it. We may look at the mountain we must climb to get it as too high. Then, as a means to comfort ourselves, we may resort to conceding to this perceived meaninglessness simply to 'get by'.

    Instead of climbing the mountain, we may dig ourselves a hole to take shelter from the coldness we perceive coming from the world. We can make a home out of the false warmth of inner darkness. When we grow disordered or enamored with delusion, we can come to incorporate harmful and dangerous beliefs. Mental gymnastics are a common result when our morality and our ideals conflict. Our ideals, however, are not reflections of our righteousness as we would like to think. No amount of pleasure equates to equilibrium. Regardless, an obsession or reliance on pleasure can lead one to hoard it or take it to extremes. The Mind plays tricks in order to avoid itself when the Personality is not in shape to face the truths facing it. Perhaps, it thinks, if we cannot see the evil, we are not doing the evil. Maybe then, it does not exist. This is how we hide behind nihilism to protect ourselves against the confusion and the fear. This is a most natural response to protect one from a world of chaos. This is what is happening en masse today. I do think the common man, and most of Man, would prefer that things see no destruction, but growth, relief and not pain. I do believe that what has been corrupted can be cleansed, made anew.

    We can isolate regulative systems in ourselves and with proper help and wisdom, start climbing that mountain. I do believe that we live in a time like no other, where the truths of our humanity are becoming increasingly obscure. But I also believe the Hearts of our people know what is worth aiming for. I do believe most feel correction is the proper response to error and that betterment offers a better pitch than decay. I believe that though not all things are entirely good or bad, efforts can incite results and outcomes that are predominantly more one than the other. We will face a lot of the same. But, I do know that in the search for this transcendence, the pursuit of this growth, that we will find much pain on its path. It requires sacrifice of our comforts, distance from our beds, and some people we must leave behind. Many individuals will be decided by the individual paths they take and the paths those paths lead individuals to. Maybe this is the 'judgment day' religions talk about. If we are to understand what, how, why, and change it, we must see how we got here in the first place. If we are to accomplish such a thing, we must journey into our inner nature. We have to come to know our Hearts. We must imagine ourselves as the animals we were before we started this whole thing. We have to come to learn what it means to meet ourselves as we were in the beginning.

I

In the Beginning

If Adam and Eve knew all the consequences of their fateful decision that damned day, do you think they would've done it? Really, if their Hearts knew all it would incur, not only the loss of their storied ignorance, but the weeping, the sighing, the gnashing of teeth, the suffering of you and me, do you think they would have chosen the same? What if they knew about the widespread aberrations from the Divine that would plague our lives? If they did, maybe then they deserve to be known as those culpable for the "Original Sin" that now stains us all. To hell with them, I'd say. Yet, as far as we're concerned, they did not have *that* much foresight. It is said they knew it was wrong, but I never read anywhere that they knew of what would occur to me or my friends or my family. It does not seem that they knew *every* single little thing that would occur as a result of their indulgence. Furthermore, what would have been of humanity's fated story if God really had no clue to the outcome of his first humans' challenge?

I would like to propose something. What if He did have foresight to their shortcomings? I think this perspective falls more in line with the qualities we have attributed to God. We know him as God for God's sake. He is said to know all, be all, see all. However, it would deviate from the traditional telling of the tale, probably far enough that priests and religious would probably start to raise an eyebrow by now. But what if it was on the course of His creation to fail in such a way? What if it was inevitable, or dare I say, even necessary for it to happen that way? What if I argued that way was on the accord of a nature God inscribed and prescribed to us, one He could not be unaware of?

So I sit here, thousands of years after the story was written, curious as hell. And as I sat there reading the holy book, I kept reading on and something about the thing seemed glaringly obvious. The whole Christian myth, from Fall to Resurrection, would not have been set into motion without the one thing Christians implore to avoid: *sin*. I thought it was an irony, really. Reading God's miracles and our graces with Him, I came to think that much of what occurred after the Fall does justice to the good derivable from making mistakes. I believe this applies even to the big ones. Without that mistake, we wouldn't have needed the grace of Christ, or those intimate moments with God like those in the biblical miracles. All of those miracles demonstrated God's 'love' for us. There would have been no prophets, no promises of salvation. If Adam and Eve had stayed straight, these opportunities for God and us to show our capacity to love one another would not have materialized. It may seem paradoxical, but I see a grand portion of the good in the world as being made possible only by the comparative evil its absence produces.

For a long time, we have tried to stop sin by waiving the threat of hell over anyone we feel stands for Sin. We throw them out of our social groups. We refuse their access to our love. We begin to behave badly towards them because we feel they deserve it. Ironically though, despite the fact that we live in a time 'beyond' good and evil, it is still very evident we very much care about the aim of some good, a 'better' of sorts. We all have our own conception of it. The thing is that the vision we have of 'better' is one that is projected by our perception from the inside to the outside and the truth is our perception is profoundly limited. We even know that sometimes, but it does not stop us. Still, we look for it. We try to enforce it where we can. We actively seek discoveries that we feel will lead to a 'better' understanding. We search for 'better' environments. The word 'better', however, can often be better represented with words like fun, exciting, different. Our tendency to misunderstand ourselves and frequently misrepresent the interior self with our limited vocabulary is daunting. We often do not know what is good for us. Those who do rarely enact a change to reflect that knowledge. We have this strange tendency to call anything outside of our comfort zones dangerous. We can even come to call them 'wrong'. Our rejection of danger reveals our instinct for self preservation. Instinct engineers us to use more caution around what we cannot identify. Our senses are fine tuned to it. The conditioning of childhood and education can engineer the brain to ignore the places where it is.

We must not confuse our culture's dispositions as our own, either. Many, in the hopes of appearing more favorable to others, reject common sense. In our refusal to see evil, we can close out that part of us where we can grow most. Because of what is around us, we can be incentivized to ignore what is inside of us. What was in the past can make us skeptical of the future. The anger of yesterday comes to show in our distaste for the present and anxieties of the future. Because of a refusal to forgive, we grow estranged, all because of a lack of knowledge. Everything has a why. Our whys are never a singular claim to a throne. Everything has a meaning, we can simply come to apply the same meaning to everything. Meanings supercharge the narrative element we blanket our actions with, making some acts very attractive and others very important. There are layers to our motives, most older than civilization. The refusal to go outside one's comfort zone is not unreasonable. It is likely because of the danger that existed for thousands of years to do so. Think of going out at night without one's group. It's dark, you know. One could get lost, lose pace with the rest, run into an animal. Our everyday fears and thought patterns reflect our genetic history, all of which are tied to our bodies and their composition as animals on this blue planet. We grew a habit of surviving, including the tendency to tell the tale. Our stories and wisdom reflect this. Imagine yourself as that hunter-gatherer, that homekeeper in those years of early humanity. Think of the trial and error one had to endure. Think of berries or fruit. We had to do a lot of trial and error in order to find out which ones would not kill us, you know? We would advise others to avoid certain fruits. I find it fascinating, friend. Maybe a connection could be drawn with this time in history, the Adam and Eve story, and the metaphor of the forbidden fruit? Just an idea. Regardless, the tone the story ends with is one of a beginning after the beginning. We chose and were changed. Our surroundings subsequently changed, too.

    The primitive cautiousness that kept us alive in those days was on display in the Adam and Eve story. Our incessant curiosity was, as well. That same draw we have to go into the unknown, the exciting, the 'more' pulled that first couple in a manner similar to how it pulls us today. Isn't it like us to want to 'know' just as children do? You know when people say that the first couple 'wanted to be like God', is it not resonant of a time when we as children wanted to be like the adults? The story tells of how we became the humans of today. It talks about the nature of mistakes, being mortals in a world we ourselves did not make. Now the great paradox is that even the wrong-doers' Hearts carried Nature's course, too. There was, however, an element of that Nature that was capable of causing harm. As a result, we all got affected because that's what harm does. While there are many more niches to this great story, like the snake and Eden, this is just a small scratch at it. There is a lot to be derived from it.

Our times, however, seem to hit logical walls when interpreting stories like these. They do not receive much consideration from most. Their context, its inherent meanings, the clothed symbols, all get set aside. They are judged by their surface. This way, Creationism and scientific understanding had a feud and some say they still do. So when we go to these tales of old wisdom, we find mythological themes, imaginary creatures, even an almighty tyrant who rains hell on whoever disagrees with 'He'. That is not pleasant to the commoner with a high school-level education nor a college educated person with a doctorate degree. Today, we have scientific inquiry and the theories of the Big Bang and general relativity. We have codes for human rights, international law, and highly sophisticated cultures. So we get to reading these ideas with the definitions and limitations of our culture and are often unable to access the perceptions that might have codified them. To that affluent Westerner, he would have to take all he does not understand in it and accept it. Without such an acceptance, he runs the risk of being labeled a heretic. Words then come to tie up a bit more than just tongues. Our beliefs get wrapped up in it.

Much of all interpretation is molded by the limitations and impressions of our words. Words are the keys to a person's Heart. One's learned definitions are like the shapes of those keys. The same word often carries different implications in different situations, depending even on the one telling it all. What means something to someone means something different to someone else. Now imagine thousands of years added on top of these barriers. For this reason, most doors in our Hearts will remain locked. The understanding of most will never be accessed because of language's failures and shortcomings. This is how we get estranged from others. So if we intend to discuss God or the mentality that drove Adam and Eve to their storied mishap, we must be in the beginning. We must understand the agency from which our actions spring and see the how's, why's and what's lying within them. This is true for any person. At the root of behavior lies the complex of intention. Roots as we know lie under the soil. So to understand anyone, one must see where they are coming from. We have to notice what it is one is lacking. We have to understand how we come to perceive something as lacking in the first place. Only then will we understand Eve and Adam or anyone for that matter. But to do that, we only have our experience to refer to.

It is interesting that the Judeo-Christian creation myth goes the way it goes. It takes us to a time when we became something apart from the world, a time where we became ourselves. To understand it is like putting the mirror to oneself. It rings of the silly way people often fail to see the obvious, mess up the simple, corrupt the good and by way of our curiosity, venture very far from our Selves. The Adam and Eve story is simple, ambitious, and profound. It tells of how we came to desire, contemplate, and acquire. That harmonized flow with God in Eden was once with us and it got lost somewhere along the way. And I think that the decision Adam and Eve made, the 'Knowledge' they sought, and the fruit they ate of and the events leading to it, was referencing something in human history. Particularly, our development. It was not just fairy tale. It was a time where we no longer the divinely protected children in the wilderness. We were now Man.

Eden was not a place, it was a time. It tells about that

transformative period when we experienced a social and egotistical transformation. The psyche as we know it was born. Our context fundamentally changed with the knowledge of good and evil, the conception of morality by those first civilizations. The whole story ends with the implication that something 'innocent' was lost. I think we came to be smart enough, sufficiently capable intellectually, to understand what we were doing. We could have lived 'in harmony' with God but we didn't. We could have been like the rest of the animals. But because of our transformative tendency and that damned curiosity of ours, we got into something we were not supposed to. We were banished from Eden, cursed to live a life outside of our Father's house.

    The Adam and Eve story tells of how we came to a 'consciousness', a level of cognitive and situational awareness, that made us unique in the animal kingdom. God prescribed us the responsibility of being 'stewards of his creation'. This was now a task we put on ourselves. Using examples of a homo sapien trying to survive, the Adam and Eve story tells how we came to be 'cursed' by Nature with the Knowledge of self-awareness. This line of reasoning can be observed in the couple's discovery of their nudity. Adam and Eve were confused for a moment, torn between the potential of the chaos or the comfort of the known. And in the face of a decision, they decided. Once they decided, they knew. And the dawn of Man's consciousness was told in a story that would resonate so well with someone of the time. We make mistakes, too. The threat that poisonous fruit and snakes posed in the wilderness, our conception of 'self', the foundations for 'danger' and 'wrong' were marvelously put on display. Once we knew, once *we understood the fact that we are*, that we live in this world, that we could never not know again. This was the beginning. When it comes to understanding the Heart, consciousness is the beginning. By it, mankind gets its uniquely treacherous, laborious, and painful existence.

Funny enough, the story goes we only needed language after Eve and Adam screwed up. After consciousness awoke in our perception, we tried a myriad of ways to describe, share, relate, and relax under the weight of our awareness. Only after Adam and Eve did we feel the need to clothe ourselves, we became image conscious. Only then did we experience 'hurt' as we know it, pain escaped sense and bled into the intangible. Of course, it did not happen overnight. We came to learn that we were destined for death through learning cause and effect. We began to feel a ways about the experiences we went through. Memory gave us the daunting reality that pain comes with childbirth and that this practice could kill you. It happened generation after generation. In a couple of those generations, we started to make the distinction between Self and Other. We were not merely reacting anymore. We began to include the past and future into the present perception. The Mind began to dress our actions with contemplation. After that, it was never the same. Just as we are beset with the reality of the inability to return to childhood, Eden remains a foggy place of nostalgia where instinct ruled. God did not kill us right then and there for our disobedience, we instead had to carry the burden of action and consequence on our shoulders.

A miraculous element of us humans is that despite losing paradise, we did not stop. We didn't give up. We didn't sit around and cry. We got to work. We began to develop words and phrases. In a world so mysterious and so brutal, we never forgot the miraculous connection between our bodies, consciousness, and the celestial junction above. We did not look at our new curse and cry about it for thousands of years. The primitive humans didn't commit suicide en masse. We made society instead. We differentiated between elements. We seasoned foods. We made tools. Our instinct yearned us to live and we basked in this instinct. Instinct forced us to pursue a 'better' and with the experience of acting on it came to see everything around us a little clearer. We saw certain methods yield desired results in greater quantities and in a shorter time. We came to prize efficiency alongside those we worked with. We included that in our understanding of 'better', as well. Our most primitive drives, those of self-reproduction and preservation, were on their way up. Make no mistake about it, we took them all the way up to the highest levels of self-actualization, my friends.

We did not limit language to self-expression. We birthed extrapersonal ideas like 'Good', even transcendental ones like the Divine. We began to symbolize, attributing tangible representations to intangible aspects of our experience that were inseparable from the material aspect of human living. We made a person out of Nature, we maternalized it. We identified with nature. We saw the world go round and round. We labeled it as God's Will. We chose to share all of these conceptions. Earlier societies wanted to ingrain these qualities into our behavior, children's minds, and our plans for the future. These terms are too often singled out and analyzed under the light of our great religious traditions, but I argue it might be worth analyzing them under a pragmatic one instead. Because if we sit for a moment and think of their *rudimentary* intentions, maybe then we give them their worth. Maybe we could even revive them to keep the spirit of their intention going. When we hear intention, the spirit of the speaker, not what we want to hear, we see past the words they use. We hear the Heart in them. We stayed closer to the tactics, phrases, and strategies that kept us alive. We called them better and named the umbrella under which they existed as 'good'. We gave these natural dispositions names, some were 'right', some were 'good'. Curiously enough, however, some were 'evil'.

    The thing is that our abilities are not perfect. Nowadays, I argue we are out of touch with a lot of things that are a very real part of our existence. We forget a lot of things too. We forget so much that I am not one to blame us for having trouble interpreting, following, or appreciating the old ideas. After all, we have so many things in front of us. But in my life and the lives of others, I find something interesting. I see these age-old wisdoms still carry their weight. These ideas do not stop at vicariously patting humanity on their back for surviving. They remind us of our terrible failures, times that made us rethink and reinforce what we really feel is right and wrong. Good, I believe, remains instinctual to us. Despite all the killing mankind has ever done and the usefulness some people see in it, it remains illegal across the world. Utility was not enough to convince us after a while. We began to punish what was 'wrong'. The weight these words carry is felt in the reason they are there: to help. We feel the weight of these words when they remind us to avoid the negative and harmful. They keep us on track, in 'God's favor'. When we are overdoing something or missing the mark, we tell ourselves and our friends this is 'bad'. We begin to get skeptical of our actions. We tell our people this is 'better' for them. We avoid what is not 'better' for us. When we do this, we advance the spirit that brought these old ideas to life on display. Our instinct can even call us to do so when we feel the things around us are not the way they are supposed to be.

    Yesterday's wisdom stands greatly challenged by the sources of information, entertainment, and pleasure we have to indulge our senses in. Not only can these distract us, they can numb us, as well. The sheer force of unearned knowledge (information), vicarious pleasure, and substantial neurochemical alteration can dull people. It can dull us morally and practically. They have the power to blind others. They may grow greedy or arrogant. To some, today's age feels like a desert and all they crave is a drop of water. We live like Tantalus, with food and water in sight but unable to get a firm grasp on it. With so much that today's globalized age offers, we can have what is a blessing to another and still feel incredibly hopeless and severely depressed. With more pornography, death, and nonsense in our hands than ever before, it is no surprise that yesterday's wisdom fails to touch the Heart in a fashion that makes it applicable, 'real', or important. This is the issue of our time, but also what makes it unique and worth living.

It is not just individuals or groups that fall victim to these temptations. The failure to reconcile old wisdom with new knowledge is one that institutions, big and small, fall victim to. These institutions include religious structures, our families, our corporations, and especially our governments. If this were not true, we would still have our first governments. These institutions are all susceptible to decay and failure when their constantly required maintenance is suddenly ignored. So those who see the effects of mass relativism, cultural nihilism, and political totalism are naturally concerned with this psychic tide sweeping our nuclear age. If all that matters is who sounds most articulate, or who looks the most attractive, or what feels best, then we might miss what actually serves humans best. The current economic and geopolitical state has exacerbated this materialistic and opulent status quo. We have a systematic tide that dehumanizes, politicizes, and marketizes too much while empathizing, sympathizing, and humanizing too little.

Our systems push us so far that we sell the bodies of others and our own. If you pick up a history book, one can read when it pushed children to labor for days on end, kept families in poverty, causing men and women to reject their dream professions. Some can even read about the evil individuals these disappointments have led to. So deflating is our way of life that our products emphasize changing our moods, appearances, and skills. Oftentimes, they only appear to do so, offering only the hope of doing so. That is enough for a hopeless populace to buy into them. Many, however, do not buy it. For those who go against this materialism, it is something of a battle of forces to preserve an authenticity, a goodness, or even a respect for the world. And for those who embrace it, it is often for distraction to relieve oneself from the weights of everyday life. The swim upstream against a materialistic life is an everyday effort to remember what is really valuable and to cherish that. It is a call to reject the vain and the convenient, to do right and to do so humbly, never forgetting one's roots nor one's responsibilities.

    We are in the beginning of an internet age. An interconnectivity unlike anything before is what history has brought to us today. So we can take a moment and appreciate that. Now, I don't mean to be *that* guy but we still have some work to do. History has not come through on making a 'perfect' populace. It has not removed the prospect of war, as evidenced by our ever advancing weaponry and some regions on Earth. We don't spend enough money on food. We don't have sufficient environmental safeguards. We still have not learned how to stop lying to one another. These facts, however, do not discourage me from recognizing that societies and Hearts around the world remain heeding and resounding the call for us to get 'better'. Tragically, we may be blinded by inner turmoil, fears, and addictions. This way, we can 'grow' but really 'shrink' as we do so. We can come to promote a 'better' that actually does more harm than good. 'Better' weapons mean more death. 'Better' drugs mean more overdoses, a greater propensity to addiction. 'Better' lifestyles can be vain accumulations of prestige. But, we often do not see this harm manifesting first hand until we reach a time that it is far too late to slow or stop them.

    It is not hard to see that most of our mistakes are made

walking that tightrope of life. We don't ask to fall. We feel the gravity pushing us either way. We are often terribly afraid of stumbling out of pressure, misbalance, even by the intimidation of fear itself. Mistakes obviously include what we do, but more commonly what we do not. We may lose what we thought was permanent only because we failed to realize it was not. Interestingly enough, we very often sense when we are doing wrong. It is one of our most accentuated sociological qualities and other people are in on it, too. That only convinces me further of the potential of a shared envisionment of a 'better' way. We get checked interpersonally, intrapersonally, culturally, and socially. It happens all the time when we are in public. People want to make sure of our intentions. It's the animal part in us that is shooing away threats. But Man uses the gauge of others too often when it comes to identifying threats and mistakes, ignoring the gut feeling within that something is wrong. Now, we can see even more room for disagreement here, especially with the fact of all these new sources of information and new angles of interpreting men and women. This is where cultures break down into smaller and smaller facets. With so many subcultures, online communities, and cultural discrepancies our markers of righteousness conflict, sometimes very violently.

    Talking about my belief for a 'better' world puts me in a spot. I run into the issue of all the world's conflicts, economic exploitation, racism, greed, and intolerance. How can we bring ourselves to believe in an inherent righteousness when Man must account for all of *that*? Perhaps this is where we can and do distinguish those who may be fools, cowards, narcissists, sociopaths, empaths, innocent, dangerous, and immoral. This is also perhaps how we can see who among us is really our friend. In some situations, we do not regard what others and ourselves explicitly deserve. We may go after what we want without regard to whether we have done anything to earn it. We disregard property, but often defend it vehemently for our own sake to preserve our ends. We may pursue what we want relentlessly, excessively, and dedicatedly, while running opposite of what we need most, hurting ourselves in the end. In order to balance the abstract, which cannot be balanced, we conceived this thing called 'fairness'. And this fairness is based in a reciprocal relationship with the conditions two individuals agreed to when dealing and interacting with each other. We obsess over fairness in transactions and relationships. In fact, what we find 'fair' forms the backbone of our globalized society. What is unfair is often what ends friendships and brings down governments, sowing the seed for tyrants.

The evil person stands out, often they take the form of tyrant or deceiver. They are not exactly doomed, either. It is not that value or worth is not present in their perception. It merely too often that their perception has been tragically misapplied. The determination of who is evil is concluded by the group, for the group, with the contribution that person makes for the group being the most prominent point of consideration. The selfish person struggles or refuses to enter a sphere that breaks the mold of self. The self is rigid. The person refuses to acknowledge their primitivity, their commonality with other people. As a result, their interests reflect this disabled perspective. They don't get along with others, they can't see what's so interesting about what's around them. Attention comes to be dealt out of them senselessly, harmfully, recklessly, excessively, to selfish ends. This is the evil that gets recognized. When we are 'wrong', we are wrong because we failed to 'meet a mark'. An imagined trajectory did not go to plan, a target was not reached, we didn't give it our all. The complex of intention did not yield the desired harvest. From here, we get the old Greek/Abrahamic idea of *hamartia*, Whatever it was that was 'supposed' to happen, did not. Whatever was supposed to happen in small amounts happened in too great ones. But I argue, who decides the mark anyway? This argument is one the moralist must contend with in our relativist age. The truth is that in our everyday interactions, we do. The mark comes from this 'place' we call the "Heart". It sets the target for our etiquette that measures out whether a designated and coordinated effort is worth it. Keeping and kicking off all the great hero stories, it starts with the target each Heart sets out to hit.

What we feel is wrong is dependent on the contents hidden in the shadow of the light of what we think is right within. Thing is, we have a laughable understanding of what is wrong. It's not that we don't feel what is wrong or haven't built systems to guard against it. It's that we can't really articulate why it is so and we get very touchy around its causes, circumstances, and consequences. We rarely understand it ourselves. To talk about problems activates a great deal of many people. We feel wrong is something to be judged for. For one, our 'sins' are not great offenses to a judgemental man in the sky. Not really. When we do something wrong, it has a lot to do with the failure to manifest our potential when we had the chance. We don't feel that we gave all we felt we should have. We didn't give enough attention here so this happened. When analyzing consequences, we can come to connect the dots back to us and this is often a painful realization. We see that we did the 'wrong'. Many make a habit of avoiding this reality check. That pain we feel to be the ones culpable is one that reflects the relationship we have with ourselves. To miss out or lose something we cared about is like a betrayal we entered ourselves into. It hurts to be in the state of rejection, especially when our actions were the ones that led us to be rejected in the first place. This way, we reenact the Adam and Eve story again and again and again. We are banished from the state that was before we ate the forbidden fruit. We long. Desire looks not forward, but back. The emotions of guilt and shame are associated with this phenomenon. Remorseful thinking, regret, painful emotions, and the works are all reflections of a 'righteous' conception internally neglected.

    The fact that we experience this does not immediately mean we are in some way pardoned or less participatory. Many confuse remorse for penance. This is yet another 'fall' on life's tightrope. We either got closer to 'losing' or 'lost' something altogether. The wretched suffer greatly. The pathetic never improve, they remain demanding and dependent like neglected toddlers or a lonely baby. One's internal dialogue can lose its linear tendency, it can become divorced. We can grow confused by who's talking in our psyche, who is who. The judgment one places oneself is powerful. After all, it is the same instinct that is pushing you to keep you alive. It almost feels like an entity, but it is all within you. It speaks to you almost like a better self. The urge to righteousness struggles in the person that cannot right a past wrong they know to be wrong in neglecting correcting. Our internal dialogue reflects that 'better' in the ideas it plants in our heads. The challenge (more like battle) to distinguish, understand, elect, and embrace our better selves is a difficult but expansive and enriching endeavor. It is lifelong. Like I said, we can prize garbage and devalue gold. But the vast richness of experience and its associated sensations and introspective revelations comprise a large part of the privilege it is to live a human life. I argue always being in touch with one's goodness is a challenge that supersedes any skyscraper we can build. To live true and honest with others and oneself remains a treasurable manner of embracing and confronting existence. The problem for most is reconciling our external reality with our internal desire.

    Nowadays, society's goals are little more intricate than

the primal motivations Man had many moons ago. But for that reason, the target is smaller and harder to hit. At least, it feels that way. Wrong seems to have come to include more, it seems to have become more 'accessible' than ever before. For that same reason, it feels like we miss the mark more often, as well. It also means we have more opportunity to do harm. Our age possesses new ways of doing the same things we have always been doing. Putting fingers on a screen can hurt someone as severely as a spoken sentence. But this way, we get the same sensations that we have always been experiencing, we just feel they are new because we have not experienced them or with the tools we possess. We grow obsessed with the means of getting these tools and honing the prestige their names are associated with them. We do not see their actual worth. The word is actual. And if we develop delusions about these tools, we can very quickly lose sight of what we truly love or care about. We forget what it is and see it for what we want it for, what it represents, or what we hope for it to be. This way, we become slaves to vanities. This is when we do the most wrong, and strangely when we think we are doing the most right. We give the most to get the most and receive nothing, trading the fire's heat for the color of its ash.

The first humans aimed at building, maintaining, fortifying, organizing, pacifying. That was at least for what it felt was 'theirs'. With every worker before us, trying to get by, there was something biological, primitive, personal, and social occurring in each and every one of them. It directed them with this 'reason'. They economized with others and dealt with desperation like us. In fact, most of their lives were far more uncomfortable than ours. Our ancestors powered through with grit and instinct, using ideas of Good and Bad to carve out a path that promoted life over death. That path led to the 'civil', the 'humane', the 'good' in Man's eyes. It built the legal system.

With these ideas, that itching for better found its facilitative medium through communication and those ideas are still here with us thanks to it. Our ancestors brought them to us. All they did was what we do now: survive. They did their best to keep going and that included taking some leaps of faith. Most of those leaps of faith achieved what we find most useful, brilliant, and brave today. Those great discoveries came about through the precarious and bold idealistic initiatives alongside the inevitable rumblings and tumblings of their mistakes.

    By the consequences of our first ancestors' efforts, each generation left our internal survival guide a little better drawn than the last. We grew from what failed, discouraging certain styles and methods. With leadership, we promoted initiative and encouraged the conditions so that those who sought it found love. We learned and shared this. Without love, we would not have shared it on to the next generation. We wouldn't have felt the need nor want to do so. We would have kept it to ourselves, but we didn't. And I imagine how that brutal animal came to be the loving Personality that resembles many today. I like to think about what they were thinking at that time shortly before we would consider ourselves human. I think of the ancestors before what would be considered 'my' ancestors. Then, I think of Man in the earliest periods of his ego consciousness and I wonder about the urge they felt to draw. Or what about the first symbols they shared, perhaps of danger, or the first tactics we used to flirt, how we got to words when it came to making love. What about why we ever began worshiping? I think of the first meanings that came to mind during those long, anxious nights in the wilderness. Understanding was not so drawn out then. But they still saw some items relevant and pertinent to their lifetimes and chose to associate meanings of their own with them. Some of these are still with us today, some are right here on this page.

We grew socially as we went along. More and more distinctions were able to be made in the form of our expression, ideals, and personal tolerations. As cognitive function grew, our conditions became more particular. We applied meanings to others and ourselves. New words were used. We grew in style collectively and individually. We developed identities to pair along with it, too. These identities embodied everyone and everything's unique capacities and affective dispositions. It became mean or pleasant to be around. One made their identity with the way they wanted to be seen by others, also by what we were. We became targets to others in this process, too. As we came to take awareness for granted, other's actions lost their simplicity. Our distrust for others grew as we became aware of what others could do. We recognized the tones and sounds others made and distinguished from them with an acute processing borne of our own experience. We distinguished and shared our distinguishments. Emotion came into the play. Economics and social expectation did, too. We became malicious. That's the Cain and Abel story. This person now was from an 'enemy' tribe. We made conceptions that brought us closer to our kin and distanced us from the foreign. This is simply a more sophisticated example of any other animal's ability to detect, sense, and run away. Just as we approached the wilderness we approached others and ourselves.

Identity worked. It strengthened our social circles' probability of survival. It brought us together but demanded we get along with the differences of a person's self-conception. Its collectivizing effect left a residue on human behavior we call culture. Identity did not base itself solely on our choices, it also incorporated those elements we are not conscious of. It included that which we come to be known for. It included the methods we use to channel our unconscious contents. If we made certain habits, we came to be distinguished by those, too.

Identity allowed us to navigate a relatively formless world. This is especially true as the abstract demands of societies began to pile up. With identity, we sewed ourselves a coat tailored to each recognizable environment. We learned to hide in plain sight. That way, others would not see the tattoos of our emotions on our faces. Unconsciousness, however, is always sensed. It cannot be hidden like a smile that doesn't reach the eyes. Identities distinguished us from others, drew and satisfied our collective impulse to belong and helped organize us among the many. They also came with a mask that has led to a new battle for us. This is the battle of today, but it started a long time ago. Personally, psychically, and socially, we advanced identity formation with experience. Our nature found it useful and encouraged these tendencies.

  They thought and spoke of what they learned. They articulated and gave names to bodily functions, natural reactions and patterns in those reactions. We bonded it all with reason. We described the nature of the bonds they formed. We identified love. We got to see all types of romantic dynamics, too. The people of then had problems of their own and managed with reason, emotion, and contemplation, just as we do. Perhaps greatest of all, they found out how they could get along. We caused war, but we built cities, too. We did what worked for us. What we see today is the genetic storage and continuation of practices our biology has found useful. We carried it on with repetition, memorization, uniform application, and vocalization. Through their repetition, we acquired styles with overlapping meanings. In those overlaps, we formed connotations, unbelievably structuring the whole thing with grammar and tradition so that hundreds and thousands of years later, we can say we still carry it on.

  When one goes into the beginning of things, one can grab insights like these that make life all the more richer. They also make your person all the wiser and this richness is exactly what makes some societies great. They may not have had 'more', but they had an eye to make it so. They also had a work ethic to keep it so. We didn't become the world's dominant species by the size of our arms, nor the speed of our legs, but we used them anyway. Our psychic development grew dramatically by our efforts to improve. With time, those primitive humans of yesterday came to resemble the more 'civilized' people of today. From hunger, we migrated to 'make' ourselves. Making ourselves now means something entirely different. With the resources of our greater societies, we build what we can. What that means today usually refers to a positioning within society that we feel reflects our internal desires. We meet the world halfway. Through traveling, we gained new knowledge. With greater responsibility, greater opportunities to demonstrate a mastery of it. All of this is part of the 'work' we were 'cursed' to endure following the Adam and Eve story. This is life after Eden.

      Our interactions with information and definitions shape our thinking, our hopes. As intellectual architects, we make houses with the sticks of stimuli. We glue it altogether with the warmth of cohesion, frequently experienced as the mental condition of logic as derived from sense. We are logical or we are not. We fight to keep ourselves in it. Our ability to build psychically is a product of our cognitive capacity, a capacity curated to enable survival. Henceforth, it reflects our physiological tendencies. Just as we brace for the elements with physical structures, we brace for the arduousness of the inherited Unconscious with mental shelters. In these houses, we take shelter from public opinion, ego deficiencies, fears. Our identity is not simply an expressive medium, it is a tool meant to increase our odds of success within the chaos of a social group. They protect our identities and the way we think. Since we rely on these to hoist ourselves into a confidence to brace the world, we naturally will protect our identity and its accompanying reputation. Behold, our psychological defense mechanisms.

As silly or ugly as the lengths we go to make sense of our thoughts can be, they are all born of the same 'righteousness' that produced the ideas of good and evil long ago. Thought is an extremely sophisticated manifestation of our fight or flight response. In order to exist cooperatively with others, we mimic, utilize, and inform ourselves of other's expectations. We fawn. This is how we 'blend in'. Our Mind tortures us because of the way we have made human society function. The defense mechanisms seem to endorse a belief that being in a group is safer than being alone. We avoid that which we fear or deem harmful. So then, the defenses work around these fears and harms to prevent them from manifesting. They inspire us to speak in harmful fashions. We hurt others to defend ourselves. This could mean we negate a responsibility for a long time, but more often it means we try to morph our inner feelings to match the outer expectation. The problem is our interpretation of the outer expectation. Without an individual sense, culture's opinions become our opinions. If we never unravel this, we simply remain blind to the fact. We live someone else's life. It is our biological instinct to want to be accepted in the tribe. After all, strength in numbers, right? But if we can't see where the culture is blind, we will help them build the hell our later selves and children will have to go through. If you want that, then go ahead and do as you please. If not, I see it's imperative we disentangle all this nonsense before more suffer its consequences. Even with symbols, nations, and honor, it is still all primal, even though we think these are 'higher' levels of thinking.

We miss our primitivity when it is adorned with

language, culture, and custom. Ideas once intended as definitions, to enable goals and motives, transformed. They became codes of judgment, metrics for social acceptability. In reference to what was 'right', we sourced insults for those not in line with these social 'norms'. After enough generations, using the same old words, there is no experience of a time where they were suggestions. Right and wrong become modes of operation that like a vehicle takes us either back or forward. They are the mannerisms embraced or rejected in a collection of behaviors and beliefs. It is our social conditioning. Even though people follow the code does not mean they have the understanding of why we things that way. They are just social norms now. By this point, etiquette once based on right and wrong reigns in people's minds as a code to analyze and judge one another. We grade their social positioning by the homage and obedience they paid to the idols of that culture. We outsource our morality to obedience, forming a reliance on others' opinions, a reliance they can perceive and often capitalize on. Our value in the eyes of others can be compromised this way. Those who become aware of themselves distinguish themselves from all of this. Outstanding individuals often do so through an outstanding and stern understanding of right and wrong that consolidates with the internal ideals of the rest. Usually this makes the individual an outlier in society as they are unable to be examined by the common person, but that is exactly what made them 'different' from the rest. That person's individuality stands as a great offense to the one who cherishes his social positioning. Culture by this point is an enabling end unto itself by itself for the sake of itself. And when it gets entrenched enough, people no longer obey the culture's moral intentions. They know nothing of them. The obedience to the culture's expectation becomes the moral intention.

    To tame our primitivism, we pressured our peers.

Historically, we grew more intolerant. In order to protect our 'civility', our progress, we chose to separate ourselves from those cultures or practices we felt were not contributing to it. This is what tradition is all about. We appreciate our similarities and given the wilderness of life, I think it is expected for people to guard their similarities. We disagree a lot because of this tendency. It is rarely because of a real hatred of the disavowed, it is more often than not the tribal fear of becoming an intruder to others in the group that gets activated in our Minds. To be like 'that' would take from us. In some cases, everything we have. When we do not want someone in our lives anymore, we deem their intentions or behaviors harmful and classify them as a threat. We do not want to be 'that'. And when we are rejected by a lover, or a social group, or an institution, the fear of being that intruder is activated and applied to oneself. This is another element of our current struggle. Despite the connection of it all, many of us struggle and feel like we 'do not belong'. We long to belong, though. It's a thing about my human. This urgency to it, my friends, is a part of the same 'spirit' of tribalism that guided us in the jungle long ago. It is merely a manifestation of that never-escaping primitivity in one of its many varied forms. What we tolerate is structured by the dispositions etched into us by the culture we were born into, this we cannot escape.

  Cultural identity came to be one of the elements of human life we identify most with being human. It's a large part of what this portion of human history is all about. In fact, many find the course of their lives being enriched by this very phenomenon. Many leave home to explore it. Many have gone to war to defend it. Many immerse themselves in it when they want to change themselves. Many hope it will be their place to grow. It is protective and defensive, but also gives us an arsenal to go on the offensive. This is where the conflict starts. Committed to this identity, even in the way we greet other humans, our preferred language, style and method of delivery shows it. We protect ourselves from making enemies this way. With a perception of loneliness that needs assertiveness to retain our mating capability and a need for validation, we keep this culture machine alive. In that process, the old and famous states came about, all because we felt it was 'better' to steer our ship a way. Our conceptions, definitions, and social expectations continued to grow in intricacy. We no longer lived to find food, but to maintain the structures that made its presence a continuity.

We guard these institutions, especially the rationale that goes into supporting them. With word, expectation, and collective punishment, we guard them from naysayers, defamatory information, and personal indifference. Practices that were once coping strategies against the elements became tests of loyalty over time, whether through mimicry, praise, or repetition. Groups came to recognize others as with them or against them. This was the case even if some were socially ambiguous, philosophically undecided, or innocent. With social expectation, we decided what was an intrusion. Our desire, like in all mental endeavors, played a big role in this. We perceived those who existed as antagonists to our interests or barriers to our desires as enemies. The symbols we use to represent our internal deductions found some agreement and people bonded over and under them. Every now and then, they rose above them. And as emotion bled into practices and hopes, passion naturally came into the equation. Reason guided, but it only fanned the flames of our fury, leading us to believe some behaviors were 'necessary'. We found reasons to live outside of the fact we were alive. We fell in love over time and into hate when there was pain and lies. Our neighbor became the same as ourselves, until they weren't. The enemy? Below us. Empires and wars ensued.

Society is hard to defend, but it is not an empty cause. I wouldn't write otherwise. We do catch on to the stupidity and madness of things. We eventually weed out habits we held onto for emotional and personal security. We may realize they are now futile in improvement better found elsewhere. We may see they were irrelevant and harmful the whole time to what was actually right. We may have been made oblivious or have forgotten there was a 'better' way. We may be afraid of making the changes it asks of us. We may be afraid to face the lack of a practice or a person or a certain system for living. Large swathes of the masses may be afraid of that change. We may be led to believe something is not important when it is. That is okay. Others can illuminate us, reminding us of what is. But it is important to remember that just because a change hasn't reached the crowd's attention, that it is not needed. The crowd may simply be too lazy, ignorant, comfortable, misinformed, or scared to realize it and do what is necessary. The Heart always knows what the Mind does not wish to face. Our commonly unexamined neuroses, coupled with a hate of what is 'wrong' and a fear of what is 'right', produce those momentary indecisions, the lack of focus, that results in our everyday mismanagements. In fact, the path of this life is based largely out of these mismanagements.

We miss out, mismanage, and minimize great opportunities because of this complex. We make homes out of our lies. Often, doing so so we can reject the truth of a matter for a delusion that keeps a present comfort viable. We can be accustomed to a certain level of bullshit. We take the threat of chaos, psychic disorder, as seriously as physical harm. We fight it. Ever see someone get defensive? This can be imagined as someone attacking the walls and structures of our thought homes. The stronger the argument is and the more attached we are to the content of the argument in question, the more defensive we get. We trap ourselves in the excuses and consolations we offer ourselves. We get in our own way. We don't need another argument to divide our Hearts. We do not control what floats to the top of our minds. And most of the time, they are conflicting sides of our value structure. We fight for what is 'right'. We conjure up wicked pictures of the future to prepare us. We spur up emotional reactions to intimidate others away from our prized places, people, and purposes. Trauma, panic attacks, and flashbacks are all examples of this. We call them *intrusive* thoughts for a reason. Others' words often poke the hole that opens up the realm from where these intrusive thoughts spring forth. There are many signs you have entered the headspace of someone's personal attachments. Be careful there.

    Sometimes we really do have a slice of truth to offer to someone about the nature of a situation. But as previously mentioned, this is a most dangerous affair. Jesus, himself, warned no one likes someone who spills the truth. That is not because the truth is not helpful, but because it often causes us a feeling we do not like. Humans gauge a lot, determining most actually, by whatever feeling that person or phenomena inspires in us. This way, we can become quite spiteful of individuals who make us feel 'wrong'. Really, those individuals may be the ones offering us the most. Our identity, however, can come to make an enemy of Truth the same way we make an enemy of someone we do not understand. When entrenched in conscious self-deception, the Truth is the enemy as are those who one stand for it. We can grow so antagonistic towards Truth that we can come to perceive a statement as an attack. We can become hateful of those who want the best for us simply because we are afraid of the 'best' they see, the potential we know internally. The receiver may become angry with what the honest person speaks. If you ever witness this, remember that the listener's

Heart is too unstable to handle the Truth at that time. They likely rely on some idol to keep their identity afloat. Their thought home, their identity, stands on a weak foundation. When the blow of truth is too forceful, it can topple their thought homes instead of restructuring them as the truth is often intended to do. Our tolerance of Truth at any given time is directly correlated to our relationship with and to it.

Our thought homes are interesting, they shape the way we view our surroundings. The state we perceive of our surroundings is what we call our situation. The situation could be one believes too much in one's illusions, meaning the foundation is the only strong part of that internal structure. Perhaps the language one uses seeps in through the roof, corroding it. The deceptions we rely on for comfort are like weak spots in the roofs of our perception. The rain of Truth could leak inside and trigger the inhabitant. The persona can be sensitive. We will have to work with many people like this and address ourselves in the moments we fall into a similar trap. It is important to remember that when we seek help from the external, there will always be limits. Even when another offers the most relevant and accurate rhetoric, it is doomed to misinterpretation by the listener. Our instinct, my friends, always rules. We instinctively avoid pain, whether by escaping from it, trying to kill its source, or appeasing that source. And in these cases, the truth's benefits and utility are ignored to preserve the routines in place to quell the longings of the Heart.

The beginnings offer a picture for the present. Today, we too often rest with our conceptions of righteousness. By finding culpability with the guilty, feeling sympathy for the 'innocent' and defending them, we shape the expectations we employ in society. Instinctively, we make judgments to determine something as viable, safe, or legitimate. We avoid and condemn things we feel cannot be described this way. This is where we get into the more negative aspects of our humanity. Addressing the nature of those will comprise a lot of the remainder of this composition. In these situations, we often declare this or that immoral, unjust, or unfair. In order to reach those planes of understanding that will make the world better, we have to go past these sentiments. We have to see that what we think is right at any given moment will be doomed to spawn from an instinctively-fueled, improperly informed, and eternally longing perspective. Because we lack information constantly, the delusional nature of our desires paired with our inherent self interest results in the conflicts we see with our fellow man.

     Once a negative determination has been established about this or that, we are no longer on the side of objectivity. Instinct will drive the response. Our reactions to things will be not based in the 'best' case for 'success', but in the greatest likelihood of attaining the ends where we store our comfort. Our reactions will be bound to the perceived value of a certain way to act and the object we are interacting with. Our instinctive predilections will be poisoned by economic positioning and our chemical dispositions at any given time. The determinations others give us will never be the value we actually possess. We will make mistakes as we did in the beginning. We could simply be having a 'bad day'. We could also be leading a 'bad lifestyle'. We could be so hellbent on finding 'evidence' for our evaluations we become convinced of our determinations. We may rely on ourselves to understand the world, rejecting sense and reason. We can live a vicarious life, my friends. Even science can trap us as religion does. We can come to view life in such a condensed fashion that we seek to have our beliefs reinforced with each interaction. This is the egocentric way of living and it is the status quo in today's globalized age. Even in the educated, the circular nature of learning can trap us over time. Those 'convictions' of invariably old age come. But regardless of age, my friends, it is a sign of a potent maturity to remember our convictions are never perfect and to act accordingly.

Using our words, we will make our world. The world itself will be confined by the definitions we have for those words. The definitions will be molded by experience, wrapped and adorned by belief, and then applied. Because of them, we will sway to one way or another and do it to others in our assessments of them and their situations. This is where many of us get our beginnings. Ruled by the belief that one option is 'better' than another, we negate, construct, deny, and fortify our habits, systems, devices, relationships, ideals, and more in the hopes of 'purifying' them. While sensing the world, we conjure values we ascribe to certain methodologies, feelings, and circumstances. We even make these evaluations unconsciously. We make them in nearly all instances from walking down the street to meeting people for the first time. Ever notice someone attractive catches your eye? Or how your favorite food drives your senses? What we aim at is instinctive, my friends. Don't forget. Those split-second evaluations we make in the 21st century world are the same ones that kept us alive in the wilderness. The only thing that has changed are the means and methods we use to navigate the world. We have stayed the same. We remain those animals making split-second decisions in the urban wild giving the best effort we can to survive.

Man doesn't need to worry too much about such wild concerns, but his wild tools remain as instinctive and sharp as ever. While many of us still contend with the issue of thirst and hunger, many don't. Most of us do not have to spend our days worrying about the animals of the wilderness. Many of us contend with maintaining the institutions previously set up so we can continue having access to our physical needs. The concern remainsbiological. Today, the majority of our days get spent in restaurants, offices, near computers. We do not deal with survival directly, but with the institutions that will grant it to us. We rarely, if ever, activate the rush and internal motivation of self-preservation. It passively gets us by. We remain more concerned with retaining the status we are holding in these institutions or access to pleasures that ameliorate the confusion. This is what we deal with today. People will use their capacities to win, earn, and save as naturally as a cheetah uses its speed or a snake its venom. This is why we heed wisdom. We learned to think twice when observing phenomena inconsistent with a 'good' outcome. In modern man's comforts, his conscious memory is not preoccupied with getting eaten by animals. Modern man is preoccupied by the state of his social, commercial, and logistical concerns. His memory is soaked not in potential game to hunt and their strongholds, but the social movements to find gains in his modern life. The connection between our primitive abilities and modern life is still evident.

Our stories continue to try to capture this sense for the positive. Now, it is mainly done for the capitalization of entertainment The world also allows us insight to the wrongs of the past with a brand new access to the nature of the current status quo. That should make the world more sensible, right? As of now, not exactly. So how should we combat this existential challenge to our Hearts? With the beginning of this new form of being, how can we retain the urge to keep this righteous and to know what is right? As we digitize what we love and undermine the 'old', what is our next lesson? If anything, forget the future. Why haven't we learned from our mistakes to mitigate the suffering of an already difficult existence? Why are we willing participants in our own downfall? Why don't we recognize and correct the shortcomings in ourselves we so easily point out in others? How can we encourage our politicians to do the same, to hold power humbly, when we do not? How do we reach this without coming to disagreements leading to the deaths of millions? How can we embrace love when it is so hard to trust anyone? All of these are questions that came up after our divine divorce following the banishment from Eden and they are all questions that give all the more power to tomorrow.

      The sins in our lives will continue if we remain unable to see the continuity of our primitivism. And given the pain we inflict on one another, it is evident we can't afford to sideline ideas like the common good, cooperation, and tolerance. Without these, we will be unable to achieve forgiveness and more importantly, redemption. This is all, of course, if we care about preserving and proliferating the quality of human life. All of this will demand some of the harder elements of being a person, that is learning about oneself, becoming aware, learning to be emotionally in tune, but also hardened to the extent we can care. Those who do are the real heroes. It all begins with the ability to resist the world's temptations. It begins with the understanding of how Adam and Eve came to eat of that forbidden fruit. We actually become ourselves with a mitigated approach to our desires. Then, we can actually see them. This way, we can connect to ourselves again, this time not blindly. Love begins with the ability to resist. It consolidates itself in us when we find the righteous reason to do so. The story of Adam and Eve reflects the first and most prominent commandment of the Old Testament, the one that warns us of false idols. I wonder, even without this godly conception, if we can see how deeply we have been conditioned. If love is on the Other side, are we willing to try to get there? From there, I argue we can get all we will ever cherish. We can choose the good. We can make Eden again. Are we willing, for a moment, just a moment, to unblind ourselves to see just how deeply we live in a world of idols?

Man seeks to escape himself in myth, and does so by any means at his disposal. Drugs, alcohol, or lies. Unable to withdraw into himself, he disguises himself. Lies and inaccuracy give him a few moments of comfort.

- Jean Cocteau

II

A World of Idols

I have always felt everything had a hint of *strangeness*. Even as a boy, I was always wondering why I would do as I did, how I would wander where I would, constantly finding myself in conversations I felt I did not deserve to hear. Along with that, a looming shadow of regret accompanied almost everything I did. Strangely enough, with time, it became clear that I was not the 'decider' in my decisions. Instead of deciding over a desire, I instead reacted to it. In fact, the desire had a much bigger say in my decisions than my morals, principles, or even my standards. For instance, I would feel fear and immediately be persuaded to the direction of safety. This meant going to the first thing that would satisfy me. Out of the description or feeling the tone my internal voice took, I would be lured to things or away from them. Unconscious forces overpowered me constantly. My instinct had made the habit of compromising with my desires to always meet them halfway. My mind had no safeguard. Consequently, an impulsivity, a loose gate on my unconscious drives, coupled with my weakness. It made for a recipe that caused much pain far too quickly.

As much as I would like to think that control of my

thoughts and behaviors was in my will and hands, it seemed most obvious it was not. My actions did not reflect that. I did not rule myself. My ego ruled me. Despite not knowing myself, I existed, sensed, and enjoyed. Despite being so frequently disinhibited and fueled by delusion, my will was not non-existent. It was just weakened. So when the internal voice would describe me with great possibilities and motivate me to go along with descriptions, I figured my ideas were the entirety of myself and I would go along. I thought my temptations were aiming at my ideals, but they were frequently no more than a mere attempt by my mind to distract me from them. I felt that to say no was a failure of sorts. The fear of social rejection would inspire sycophantic acts. I thought they were the totality of my psyche. I decided on them in totality. I never analyzed them as separate and fragmented parts of my person. I never considered what the 'safer' options were aiming at. I went with the sense. This way, I existed selfishly. I did not realize my impulses were the 'temptations'. They were just what was 'normal' to me or what was happening' to me. I would override my real desires, which often required great change, small coordinated efforts, patience, and uncertainty. Foolishly, I replaced them impulsively with short-term certainties that assured my pleasure or relief. That way, I would not risk existing in the painful state of rejection.

I was particularly susceptible to the sensations brought on by exhilaration, excitement, and euphoria. I would calculate my actions only to the extent they worked to give me the most of what I wanted. I would work hard when I really respected a particular end. It was only on occasion, however, that I ever worked for them without self interest. When someone or something was treated right, I would get suspicious. When an institution asked for my efforts, I would often have trouble coming through. even if it treated me generously. A wrestling between some sense of duty I felt and the force of my desire would leave my perceptions bruised. I always felt the part of me that craved virtue had a more sophisticated structure than the one that led me to try to feel good. Virtue had this overarching, fruitful, intricate structure, but my passions and the narrator in my head would just never incentivize it for me. If I felt like I could get away with it, I'd proceed with my lower nature. I would choose to chase after unconsciousness. I longed for the quiet. A comfort existed there that I carved a pathway to. Instead of changing, I cowered. That quiet demanded much more if I was to achieve it in consciousness. Drinking oneself into the sleepy haze where every memory is lucid is also an easier bed to make than a real one. It carried a much higher 'success' rate with a seemingly smaller probability of pain.

     Every occurrence had to serve my security somehow. If it did not, I would make sure it was not enjoyable for anyone else. The direction of events had to clarify the uncertainty of the future for me to some degree. Whatever it was, I would rarely act in the spirit of an action. I considered only the practical implications it was affording me. I would so frequently do 'the right things' with this back pocket reason. The back-pocket reason was often the real reason why I would come to do it at all. The 'reason' wasn't ever reasonable, it would only console my fears. Many live this way. Those marked by emotional agony, mood swings, excessive mania, depressive episodes, and the like struggle with this. I spent a good number of years living this way. I would betray myself whichever way I acted. A cycle of deception and betrayal (of others and self) dominated me. I was delusional and reckless, using unhealthy coping mechanisms, heavy substance use, to cope with the destruction of my self. I would soothe myself with the same instruments that hurt me. I came to cost and take a great deal. While all I thought about was getting closer to feeling okay, I got further and further away from it in reality. The Hatred of self and intolerance of vulnerability would wrestle with my reason and win.

The play with desire was a majesty to behold. For instance, let's say I did whatever my thoughts suggested. Afterwards, we could say my reason was now free from the appetite the thought inspired. Then, I would laugh or cringe at the passion that so confidently inspired my will in the moments leading up to the consumption. I now had no appetite for it. It was mad, one thinks. I asked often what spawns such a detour of intention, noting the role of hormones in this. I began to notice just how often I did things I didn't really want to do. I noticed how in a chain of five actions, I did three or four to get to the reward of the last one. My desire would become committed to one end and it was rarely an end that had the greater outcome for my loved ones in mind. Interestingly, I noticed how worked up my psyche would get when an impediment to my wants stood in my way. In my attempts to evade rules and gain an advantage, the warpings came to include most of my undesired actions. The way I worked around limits hurt as much as they 'helped'. I came to be astounded by how cunning a person can be when challenged to work the world to achieve a desired end. I was astounded to the ends I would go. It was only until I suffered the depths of solitude that I began to put the pieces of how it occurred together.

Because of hormones, prejudices, sexual attraction, personality issues like narcissism, or Man's hunger for power, people rarely see how much foolery we walk ourselves into. We miss it. It is not that we do not introspect. It is that we often do not look until we have a mess on our hands. So while we can read our logic like sheet music, each note is like a leaf on a tree that has a trunk with roots that dig all the way down. We rarely get to the root of things, too often merely catching up to their consequential impositions. We are overrun with a lack of self-restraint keeping around habits we would prefer not to keep around. We have this tendency to keep order in the financial domains to the extent that keeps our present livelihoods intact. The rest is all chaos. Sometimes, we are willfully ignorant. We seek the relief in the avoidance, in the land of make-believe where a duty does not exist. It is a most dangerous way to live without moderation. In any arena, a lack of self-restraint is an easy to create disorder.

What we value and prioritize is the backbone of our actions, giving our understanding its stature and posture. Without the acquiescence to the presence of the unconscious, the *dark* side of the self, we will likely suffer from the cyclical recurrence of our vices and their effect on our behavior. Because we can limit our perception to the surface level, we may not be entirely cognizant of what we are really aiming at, nor why. We can ignore our true wants in the process. As we progress unconsciously in life, we will likely feel incomplete as we do so. We may become bitter because we feel something 'is holding us back'. We can lash out against others as a result. Our evaluations determine our desires. We may not realize these evaluations are largely based out of our symbolic vocabulary. If we do not disentangle our assessments, one can suffer the pushes and pulls of one's own psyche. This is largely where mistakes begin: in the misinterpretation, the poorly informed, weakly reasoned assessment. We can act out in public, in front of someone special, or say rude and manic statements as a result. We can forget to focus and we will pay the toll to one's environment or suffer the consequences. Some mistakes that disregard others are menial, others are not. Small examples of this are failing to say hello to someone and big ones something like spousal infidelity or an incident of violence.

Failing to remember what matters is dangerous. Even momentary failures to prioritize can have drastic consequences.

They ruin marriages, cause wars, end lives, and so on and so on. Momentarily and decisively, a slip is enough to change a conversation, a country, frequently doing both. So when we are deciding, where is our head really? I argue we still do not really know. All the while, human society is likely to remain dependent on that special psychic process of decision-making. Decision-making is where we meet the world halfway. We exist in a state where our actions and lack of action exert a force on the world beyond our control. In a flow that moves on its own, we are the ones who have to swim to stay afloat. The form that results from our decisions is the mold that will shape the decisions of later on. These are consequences. They determine a lot of what we are going to leave behind in this life. Because we elicit effect as people in all we do and do not do, we are deemed 'responsible' for what is expected of us. We can embrace and satisfy those expectations or reject them with neglect. They can pile up, especially if they are not immediately addressed. We take comfort in the polite dismissals and ignorable tensions. Assessments get repressed into the unconscious and a darkness follows those who harbor it. Things get hazy, things start to bother us 'without' reason, but there is a reason for all the mess.

Occasionally or constantly (depending on how you look at it), an unnecessary change in the world is caused by the execution of our desires. Maybe, just maybe, it is a change we did not want to see or even imagine. Because our actions are driven by natural and premeditated intentions, we are the ones who can answer the why and how for that unwarranted change. I want to enforce this idea. We are indeed responsible. It is one that took me far too long to embrace. In these cases, we gauge mistakes off of their reflection on one's internal value system. Mistakes are shortcomings, whether it was being late, failing to call someone back, or not doing your taxes. Our actions and reputation fail to reflect the desired appearance and hopeful quality of our behavior. The identity is hurt. These kinds of changes can traumatize us and leave us scarred. In some cases where accidents occur, much guilt and disorder can be incurred. In some cases, we suffer as much as the victims, caught in the crossfire of consequences now due to us. Each player in this theater has their role in the Story.

Sometimes, culpability is extended by omission or even transferred over entirely because of it. An action can be forced onto a person, they could have been instructed. Another could have waged something of immense value to that person, or blackmailed them. This way, perhaps we were not in a position to choose well, lacked the wisdom, or were made to feel indecisive by those around us. I have observed this in all people and in all arenas they associate. Whether in fits of anger, or drunken recollections, realizations about long-term failures, limits, I find an ability to relate to people on various fronts to the reality that humans are not perfect. Our evaluations are faulty and we fail to correlate our actions with the intention that inspired them. We can be quite foolish. *I realized the sense of my foolishness was caused by the overestimation of the value of my desires which were not comparably worth negating.*

The strange thing is that when I thought I had the most control was the time when I was furthest from it. I would delve myself deeper into my rejection of consciousness. The unconscious chains grew in strength. This way, if I failed, I would comfort myself with delusions, through minimization of the important and glamorization of the vain. The more meticulous I was in seeking what I wanted, the less in control I had. The more I gave to the efforts of getting what I wanted, the less I had to offer to the world. After all, I was only thinking about myself. But I thought these deviations were in my best interests, part of *my* world, yet they were only illusions that defrayed the interests of those who *really cared*. Their tears did not change me. I kept tugging on them to get away from the effects I was eliciting. I never accessed the control I did have until I stopped chasing those sources that I thought were giving it to me in infinite amounts. After a while, I saw the only control I did have was simply my ability to decide. I also saw that even that was ruled by the primal, social, cultural, physiological, and historical pushes and pulls that led to me experiencing them presently. When I saw how powerless I was, unable to rule even myself, I had to ask why. Where did it all go? Why does it even leave in the first place? Who was the judge in my heart? Why did I exist in dread, repeating my self-destructive cycles, failing the ones I loved? What were the secrets behind the shapeshifting of my heart?

      Much of that shape shifting occurs in order to please our idols. We look toward society as a frame of reference for what is good or not. We look to situations similar to ours and compare. We get our cues from those around us. While a useful tactic, it can backfire. We often make the habit of making room for those things our societies value. Our societies have provided us with structures of value that aim against unnecessary pain and suffering. This has kept us alive. But what exactly is the goal of our trends, our styles, our heroes? If we think today is all that ever has been, we will experience the mistakes of the past as novel experiences. We reset or hinder the advancement of wisdom, multiply suffering, by failing to see the past. One who has no understanding of the past lacks the knowledge to see it repeating itself. We give a great deal of value to efforts and institutions that do not really value us. So I ask, what is the goal of our appreciation, admiration, that worship of superstardom? We could go as far as we want in any stretch, but what is the end goal our societies are aiming at? Who are we worshiping in our lives? What do we deem the most desirable and what makes it so? Why do we feel the need to get there, why do we feel the need to imitate it? If all the lights can blind an individual's relation to common sense, imagine a society's.

Our actions spring from our ideals and those ideals carve out the shapes of our idols. The idol is our placeholder, our way of vicariously experiencing the consolidation of the hopes we have for ourselves. Culture simultaneously shapes what we want to be while remaining the funnel we seek to achieve that vision through. This culture machine will keep doing its thing. So the iPhone is not the end, TV shows are not the peak of art. Our celebrities are not perfect beings. This is not the greatest we will ever be. It is not evil to make goals. The issue lies when we make a goal or routine that actually deviates us from our potential instead of actualizing it. Far too often, we outsource our best ideas to someone who will not take it to Heart. Or, we place our trust in someone to speak for us because we respect their ability to articulate. Many times we will have this set of reasons, this list almost, of explanations for the subservience we tell ourselves is worth enduring. These can be reflecting a betterment of self, but that could be a farce. It could just be that much of what one aspires to is meant to quell the longings of Wholeness or healing in a person's Heart.

The human society exists as it does because of its idols. Every day, idols drive the world's contents, shaping the expectations of our households and international diplomacy. Some do get to decide on behalf of many. Many idolize such a position. But we must not forget nearly everyone gets the blessing of being able to control at least one, that is oneself. So many are worked up to high heavens with this obsession with controlling others. This obsession is rarely an end, mostly a means, but it can definitely be an end in some cases. Regardless, I argue we have enough on our plate with ourselves. In this world of idols, our weaponry includes our ability to recognize, intuition, memory, pattern recognition, inference, induction and deduction. We got to where we are because of these invisible weapons. They drive intention. Without intention, the human would not be that cunning primate that creates stories, that deceives. It also would not be the idolizing animal that we are. From these aims we see drives consolidate themselves into a generalized, specified, or idealized direction. If only it were stable and consistent, right? Even the disciplined person will tell you the voice of intention that like a buoy on the ocean's surface sways back and forth, tucks in and exalts out, or remains stable until the conditions strike. I argue those consolidations are our idols and this world is full of them and they compete a lot. They battle for our attention and they constitute our internal turmoil and temptations.

Intention drives our idols while also fueling them. It allows for a uniquely clever way of acquiring our needs and desires. It is one of the most significant factors of how we got to the top of the food chain. It is a remarkable human ability, allowing us to string objects of our perception together to paint a canvas that leads us to thrive as a species to an unimaginable scale. As humans evolved and their psyches grew in maturation, they gained greater control of their intentional abilities. Humans use intention to mitigate disasters of natural and unintentional origin. They use it to get food, plan out the day, exercise, administer drugs, relieve their large appetites, and even complete small goals in the perceived progression towards a bigger goal. Intentions can be shared or pushed on others. And much of culture is built this way, through the insistence of the past and the fear of collective punishment. The pressures the individual faces in the face of collective demands leads to an acute state for the socialized person. As we all scramble to get what we can from this world and the resources some own, we get crafty. From here, we get the practice of *persuasion*. It is another's attempt to secure the needs of the idol. The world is full of this, too.

We can idolize culture itself. Being social animals, we love to belong. *Much of culture is built on the imitations of formerly successful attempts to survive.* After a while, we can forsake its utility and continue doing it solely because others do. If an act is normalized and others have embraced it, we can suppress our aversion to it for the group's sake. We can make a habit of this repression, too. Habit forms much of the fabric that constitutes culture. We think we pioneered culture, but most of it is merely a repetition, reinforced by the conditioning of education. With conceptions of 'normal' and 'righteous', we justified our governmental and religious power. While these concepts carry symbolic weight, that weight is often not what is transferred when they are used. Righteousness is frequently morphed into a frame of reference to distinguish people's standings in a group. After all, we have to understand, right? As we vie for information, we get together with the sources we trust. This is how social groups form. Then, carrying on with the information we received, we decide whether we 'like' people or not. We grow expectations, wants, and plans with our mental mapping. Navigating the social world, we decide which and who is worth what, what risks are worth taking. Some of these risks run contrary to social norms. In these cases, we make idols for ourselves. We distinguish ourselves.

The miracle is that in order to have achieved what we have, we actually had to agree on some off these idols. For society to function, we have to come to some consensus about what is desirable, attractive, useful, logically possible. The miracle is we did, en masse. Culture is everywhere now, everywhere we turn. Every home has become its own culture. The sad truth is, however, we can grow dastardly confused with so much to indulge in. Mind has separated Man from himself this way. We adore what we do not need. We chase money even though if offers no natural nutrition. You can't eat money. Our social system works off it, it has a price for everything. For this reason, not for the sustenance of the body but the idea of the possibility of getting to do so, we chase it. Because our needs have been enveloped by our obsession with money, that chase for it becomes as necessary as a hunter gatherer wandering the wild. I am not saying money is wrong. However, when that system has embraced methods that actively disorganize the self, pin one against another, trapping others, we have greed. We do this for our idols and because our idols differ, the energy greed consists of is not limited to money. Anything that is useful, aesthetically pleasing, demanding, or complicated can possess and compromise our value system if we are not careful.

On social media, people give us a timeline of this possession live. We get a picture of our society's psychic condition. We get to see what and how it idolizes and the consequences of doing so. Other's conditions give us a feeling about ours. We experience without the trouble of consequence this way. I find it no surprise that more sexually suggestive imagery tends to increase the attention something receives. The more bodily the ambition, the higher the probability it will be appreciated by another. It plays on what the body has been engineered to do. The elements that make us unique with a personified impression, made to last over time, have no relation with the body. They are related to our sense of self-esteem. Many sacrifice this sense to another's desires. What we would not have done unto ourselves, we may have allowed others to do to us. They lower us internally. Our culture is soaked with these 'lower desires', more common, easily birthed, hormonally entrenched and inspired. A sexualized culture plays on these pulls. So on the internet, tips to elevate one's status and efforts to do so are rampant. The status seeking we have always participated in has taken new form. So tips for making money, makeup tutorials, promiscuous dancing, and celebrities (excluding cat videos) tend to dominate social media outlets.

In our world of idols, these dogs push their agendas onto us. They do this often because they can, but mostly because they feel the need to do so for one reason or another. We are the dog, too. Lord knows I have been the dog. I have been before and I very likely will be again. The spawning of desire within the person, like appetites that call for satisfaction, comes to emit a force and the effect it has on the consumer leads them into the hands of a producer's wiser response to those cravings. All they have to do is stick the net and we'll be the fish going right in. How strange is it that people change their life's orientation, their belief systems, morals, customs, mannerisms, and much more out of the mere *prospect* of getting what they think they want! All the while, we expend more time and effort to get farther and farther away from our natural needs and closer to artificially constructed games whose ends have no end!

And there are positive, highly insightful contributions on our new mediums, this I will not deny. But I think something tragic occurs when this exploitative material overrides our artistic instinct. Or worse, when commerce deludes the art. Some videos play on the primitive drive to be the biggest dog in the pack, the reproducing dog. Others seek admiration for their lifestyle. These are all power grabs of sorts, small and large. Our vanity increases when we see just how big other's vanity can be. Some people try to make us jealous, particularly by flaunting what others are generally known to want. The incentive to act these ways is as primal on the screen as it is in person. The need those pulling the strings feel to do so are too. They are all attempts by the person posting, speaking, or plotting to advance the imagined conception of self, to actualize it. Social media offers the opportunity to expand this conception like never before. The fact remains, however, that some conceptions illuminate while others darken. It is silly to believe all idols are created equal. The internet has been excellent at demonstrating the primitive philosophies of tribalism and all-for-one attitudes. It has ballooned and will keep doing so, with unfathomable imaginings on potential modifications to how people do business and conduct themselves. It has made currency plastic and the justice system a virtual experience to behold. Online communities, especially ones that seek privacy due to the depravity of their viewing pleasures, have proliferated and are creeping into power. They can be political, religious, and xenophobic in nature. Even governments themselves work the system to their ends. They pose through conventional social media platforms, spreading the propaganda. The foolish and naive person gets pulled into their line of thinking unknowingly with a meme, or an emotionally exploitative poster, a moral appeal. All of this happens at any given time on the internet. All to make one side of a political aisle, a lifestyle, a culture, a pocket more appealing than the other. Even if one were to bring their reason to the digital world, it would be as though one stood with a lone bottle of water in a desert.

    We put on filters, we alter. We lurk, a consequence of our rumination. We see the final product and reject the way it reflects us. It would violate our standing with the idolizations we have made. The power of the internet is its ability to propagate our social tendencies without anyone being in the same room. One may even be led to change their beliefs, political or non, by the incessant pull of other peoples' posts. The respect one places on a person's knowledge does the same. We can all of a sudden become attracted to people with a pleasantly looking image when we do not really find them attractive in person. Then, when in the room with these people, the ball game changes. The Mind does not do well with contradictory beliefs. The platforms disturb the pace of our minds with all the persuasions it attempts to get over on us. They stress us out. We could become addicted to differing sources of information and entertainment. The devices latch on to the portion of our psyche that is vulnerable to repetitive, skeptical, and inflammatory stimulation. The issue is that all of those things affect us in many ways we might not see but I am sure we all feel.

We should not underestimate our idols. We should definitely not be blind to them. We should not be afraid of how ridiculous they are either. That is how we get into trouble. In order to spot them, one has to be aware. So when thinking and feeling and wanting, I look at the particular contents of a thought, feeling, or object of desire and try to notice their overarching direction. I ask, where are they trying to get me to? They are, if not always, rooted in the body. I may not 'feel good' or 'feel comfortable'. Then, I remember what the body wants. Our idols come out of our primal goals. Idols distinguish people. First, we assure safety. Then, we seek to understand something to find out our level of interest in it. Then if a person, place, or thing's features seem more and more helpful in helping us reach our idols, our attraction to it grows. Then, more attention will be placed on it. If something is simply not worth one's while, one will see it as simply not worth one's while. If a career has benefits, a high salary, a high amount of vacation and sick days, flexibility for work-life balance and so on, we will like it. It serves us. With the more 'assistance' we perceive as coming out of an item, the more we will appreciate it. We seek growth, progress and increasing intrication. We like what we feel will give that to us. We detest what we will feel will get us away from it.

Just because they become accepted does not mean all idols are helpful, even cancers grow. Idols grow from our attention. Ideas grow, progress, and become increasingly intricate with their adoption, application, and acceptance. With their rejection, ideas like plants without water, wilt, wither and die. Being social animals, we give power through idolization. We do it for a plethora of reasons. The most competent or popular usually reigns here. Our lives will be determined by what we give power to. Our lives will be saved by what we take power away from. We get the choice of which idols are worth our time and which ones are not. The ideas we entertain come to be the flavor we taste life with. They become the responses the body grows accustomed to undergoing. The responses become the decisions that lead to the outlook we give to our children. All because of what we idolized in this world. Are we really going to be a generation that, like some cancer, leaves a weaker organism after making a home in it? With the filter of human reason, one can actually make the choice to stop serving that tyrannical king within.

    The question must be asked. Where do we begin when we have the nuclear warheads pointed at one another, bombs capable of pulverizing entire communities of humans? How do we get to a world where people aren't deluded enough to send out such a thing? In order to explore how, we must begin in the beginning of our perceivable thought streams. We must work from the point we are at. What we have and lack in this moment carries clues about *how* we have been and that is seen in the idols we've had and hold, the aims we've conjured out of those idols. This way, we get an understanding of the inclinations of our interpretations, the biases we have normalized and been limited by. If we never see them, we handicap those who are under our tutelage. The Truth we reject in ourselves is the truth we cannot be relied on to offer. Facing it when others are not capable doing so can be unpopular with the group, but there is power to be yielded from it. This way, we can take a step back from the preset evaluations society gives us about what success is. This way, we can determine which victories are worthwhile, and form some of our own.

Because as magnificent as our cognitive abilities are and as grand as the scenarios they offer may be, they are not perfect. One can argue they're not even real. Not only can our perception be swayed by information from the physical world, biases and complexes will, like shot gears, negatively affect the final product. And when cultures collide, it will be because we did not like the meanings we have for the words the others were taught to use. We may just see that all we need for peace is to realize our intentions are not very far apart. People, even as we pile layers of so-called "awareness" on top of this consciousness, are still slaves to it. We follow people when we want something. We find some things interesting and others boring. We get irritable when hungry. We form narratives out of the absurdity of all things existent. We make stories of people, places, and practices, place 'ownership' on things, individuals, and ideas, and much more beyond that. This is all a part of our nature and it is what makes our idols. And these are not new, they have powered life since before we made civilization, since before this planet was blue. What we are is perfect but who we think we are is not.

In a world I find so strange, do we have to be strangers to ourselves? Do we have to be strangers to others? In running away from our past, are we not becoming strangers to ourselves? We leave ourselves alone. In our newly equipped world with ample digital, nuclear, and globalized devices, our psychic workings seep through our screens, words, and cultures. I do not find this strange. After all, they are extensions of us. Instead, I find an awareness of how they affect us to be of great pertinence. If we are to have a society whose aim is not to gain more than the other, instead to help the other, we must understand how we come to want in the first place. In a democracy riddled with identity politics, we will not get very far if we stop at our idols. We need to *critically think*.

I like to think there is a reason staying away from false idols is the first commandment in the Abrahamic religions. We think it is important to remind ourselves that every human grapples with the suffering of this life. That just because a person identifies with a certain aspect of culture does that mean that is the entirety of that person. If you see a person consistently define themselves by that culture, however, you know what is like going on. Regardless, we all get hungry. We all wonder. We all enjoy and like the freedom to do so. If commoner and noble alike fail to scratch the surface of their reality and remain obsessed with the expedient differences of one another, I believe we stand to lose a divine way of life. And even if our lives had no divinity in them aside from all the hints telling otherwise, a divinity could remain in a love we conceived. Perhaps we can become free because we had the courage and foresight to refuse to bow down to false idols. A love could remain for what we were, for how we did, for who we became in light of our circumstance. But before we can get into any talk of divinity, we must rise above those rhythms that keep us in spirals, that keep us speaking, but never acting. We must learn how we enslave ourselves to these idols, how we get carried away by persuasion and deception.

"...this is the sort of thing I think oratory is useful for, Polus, since for the person who has no intention of behaving unjustly it doesn't seem to me to have much use—if in fact it has any use at all..."

- Socrates

III

Persuasion and Deception
(A World of Idols Part II)

I remember being 4 years old and standing in a line alongside the other children in preschool. I remember lying about the place of my birth to one of them. Strange lie. A child and rudely I might add protested, denying my claim, I remember I went on a tangent so long and so elaborate that it put him into submission. That was that and we carried on. The issue never came up again. No one ever asked. No one cared. However, this was the first time I remember ever being intentionally deceptive. That tangent was the first time I recall ever attempting to persuade anybody. Over the span of my short life, I have told thousands of lies, perhaps tens of thousands. I have been intentionally deceptive to hundreds of people to some degree or another. Furthermore, I have failed others hundreds of times, maybe thousands of times. I have been a conniving, ruthless, and cunning human being. I existed this way in all aspects of my life for the vast majority of my years. Since I could remember, I have persuaded and deceived.

Using eloquence, I took pride in dismantling the others' arguments. In victory, I found a short-lived reassurance with the compliment to my capabilities. I had partners with whom I channeled my weaknesses, chaining them to my complexes and the ethical ambiguity that tends to result from them. I lived in egregious excess. I lied so often I swear there were some days I did not say one truth. I distorted my definitions so far I eventually forgot who was who and what was what. I negated those who loved me in favor of those places that helped me forget I hated me. I arrogantly made claims to territory. I included people, ideas, habits, and opinions in this territory. My weaknesses, too. In the defense of these weaknesses, I was rude, callous, wrong, and even cruel with indifference. I lived amorally. And through it all, I used the gifts that should have been invested on advancing some good in order to reap small and vain gains on life's playing field.

My heart was filled with vanity. I aimed at what would bring me the most prestige, the most attractive partner, the most sophisticated aesthetic. I compared myself to many greats and contemporaries and rested with ideas that compared, inflated, and bolstered my intellectual power. I would lie at my behest, taking all that was given while giving only a fraction in return. I cozied up to individuals that gave me an upper hand. I have used charm since boyhood to escape the consequences of my actions. Having the gift of oratory, I grew evermore vain as I excelled in rhetorical competitions. I enjoyed the fact of being enjoyed. I really did. I thought somehow by doing all of this I would 'stop losing'. I was the one who was confusing enjoyment for progression.

It was not until I faced a sufficient enough blow to knock me off my feet that I ever felt the force of my deception come back to bite me. It was until I could no longer feel the love of someone that I loved who suffered deeply by my deception. It was when eyes that once adored me looked back at me with coldness, suspicion, hesitancy that I realized I destroyed something precious. I was walking around like my shit didn't stink. It was when I figured the costs of my vices and compared them to the cost of things I long complained about not having. It was only when I saw the foolishness of my ways, when I was driven to sleep on a strange floor with strangers, with anxiety attacks brought on by the horror of my callousness all under the umbrella of severe addictions and withdrawals.

I recall having no money. I remember the shame I felt being around my partner at this time. She thought I was unhappy to be with her or doing what we were doing, but I was actually unhappy to be there as I was. I remember we would walk around the stores and I would never smile, I would only look at the price tags while she would appreciate the product. Poverty elicits this effect. A lack of funds makes one feel deficient. The sight of my deficiency made me long for items that blinded me to it. I was not innocent, the world had no fault for me. I didn't appreciate much for a long time. I utilized my friends and family. I put them at odds with myself. I frequently overextended myself through vain projects intended to prove my capabilities. I rarely completed them. I came to be without the friends I used to have. I made a bad name for myself. I roamed far from where I started. I soiled a precious union or two. And in regards to my goals, I was running in the opposite direction. During one of those many lonely nights, in my loneliest loneliness, that vanity died and so did that shameful boy.

During my adolescence, I largely avoided peering into the roots of my deception. I see this was probably my way of keeping my house of cards from collapsing. This unwillingness to introspect reflects my attempts to keep my integrity intact so I would not live outside of my moral boundaries. I lived through the lies, spent my days under the sun maintaining their believability. Despite my best efforts, my house of cards did fall apart, from the roof all the way down to its foundation. I was blind to the harms I was causing, the dignities I was affecting, the dreams I was crushing. Above all, I was betraying the Man I wanted to be. These ways I am culpable. I lied. For the longest time, I saw great utility in it. I would sharpen those I cared about with the same tactics of rhetoric I employed on them and myself. I would preoccupy myself with honing and improving their psychic strength and persuasive abilities. I wanted them to be 'sharp' like me. I figured this would shield them from the misdeed and deception in the world. In my efforts to remain strong and successful and promote these 'virtues' in others, I would communicate the tactics I used to 'win'.

But when I finally stopped, I saw the lying for what it was. It was all a projection, for one. But, it is also my way of affecting my surroundings with some degree of control. The lie took reality in a direction that I was comfortable with. This way, I would never have to be vulnerable, like my soul laid out to be roasted by the heat of the truth. It was my way of tolerating the intolerable in me. I used it to cope, to calm the storm. People do not tolerate being lied to for long. A few gathered the strength to push back against the tyrants in their lives, some of those lives had me as the tyrant. I had to earn my understanding. I used deception tactfully and strategically, all of it coming from the shadow within all to ensure my 'win', all owed to the fact I felt I could not trust others. I didn't know how to and did not take the risk of doing so. While I sought to make others better, what I could offer were only machinations from my dark side, all I was in touch with.

Anxious and deluded I went about my days, jumping from place to place to secure my relief. And with great shame, I would work tirelessly to hide the extent of my disease. I would restrict access to others about my whereabouts, my doings, my habits, their frequency and more. I would strategically use smiles to hide in plain sight and when threatened would callously undermine others' psyches. The urge was at times terrible to say atrocious things. Whatever energy I did not expend in propelling cruel language, I used to dig into my target's deepest insecurities. Afraid of what others could do, I would premeditate the trajectory of events with people's tendencies in mind, reaching timings and accords in my favor. With an awareness of others' resources, I made myself useful and convenient to have around. Through social acceptance I found some relief, the reality of solitude and internal disorder would disappear for a moment. This is why I partied a lot. It was only until later that I realized I was giving my best to people who wouldn't think of me twice. I did not seek to include those who thought of me as so strong, not in those arenas I knew were my weakest.

The more and more I deceived, the more my mental health deteriorated. I began to suffer from profuse rumination. My lifestyle enabled this. Deception requires one to keep thinking. This is because reality begins to behave interestingly in the deceiver's mind. To the deceiver, a past event is subject to influence by a current event and vice versa. In this sense, when a liar is faced with a fact that threatens their lie, the Mind can come to perceive the truth as an enemy. It can view the past the same way if one retains one's regrets. The motive to deceive isn't always quite clear, but however it is reasoned, it is ultimately an attempt to evade or hide. For me, lying gave me a sense of temporary control in the direction of reality. Over time, all that control slipped away. Despite my ego's most strenuous efforts, Nature restored itself. My Heart would strike me with anxiety so that I would turn to face my internalities before something unfixable finally happened. My subconscious tortured me for my sins and the inevitable eventually came.

As I read between my violations of others' boundaries, recalling my memories, sensing what I felt was right and proper, I reconstructed my relationship with myself, my God, and my beloved. Losing what I loved, being alone, I learned what it was like to love myself. I imagined what I would love to receive and learned to give that to others. I would fantasize about going back and having been that person, that person I longed to be for those who deserved it. The truth was I was not. This way, I lived out my own miniature version of hell, being taunted by the delusion and being shocked at the oppositional reality of it all. With the realization of my transgressions, I learned to gauge where I walked better. I aged months in days as I did this. The recklessness in my actions began to subside and though I was riddled with anxiety, my impulsivity began to pass, too. My power to resist grew and I redefined the approach I took to myself. I shed over tens of thousands of tears. My archetypal and internal complexes, along with my economic conditions made my path seem long. I would fantasize about having what I had lost while the dreams of what I never had felt as though they were slipping farther and farther away. This is where I felt a lot of my pain.

    From the symbols I drew out and the meanings I chose to see, calls of 'righteousness' ignited my urge to fight. But because my fight was fought for the causes I prized, they remained dependent on the idols I had in mind, those I made out of the situation. So despite trying to start over, I fell numerous times. As hard as I tried to get right, signs that I was not came to rise. The trouble was that my 'righteousness' was naive. Just because one's intentions are good does not mean they will end up in good places or remain doing exclusively good things. I was often wrong in my interpretation. My obsession with goodness was a result of my fear of the alternative. Nothing got better immediately. In fact, most things got very difficult. As I came to hate who I was, that hate got channeled into instruments that were involved in my degeneracy. I spoke ill of those that 'were the way I *was*' . But I began to think of the patterns, connecting the old wisdom with my experience. What could my mind fight if it could not even see itself? Would it not be fighting itself with everything I said in everything I spoke about? Here, I finally fought a worthwhile fight. I had to ask myself, for once, if I was wrong. I had to deconstruct what I thought was right. I had to see I was still a child fighting, reflecting where I came from, what I was born into, and what I picked up along the way. The enemy was not desire nor the ones preventing me from getting what I desired, it was hidden in the reason I desired it in the first place. The manifestation of that fight would be going deep into myself and turning over all my words and actions. As I turned over that leaf, I saw my sins.

This is what I saw. I realized I negated the components of my life that required meticulous attention, choosing instead to indulge in my senses, my egocentric identity, sharpening my abilities of persuasion. It was simple and harmless, I thought. I used whatever adjectives I felt were relevant, finding it important that my tongue have rhythm in every situation. I would speak in line with the heartbeats of men and women, pacing and picking my words delicately. I appeased their egos. I absorbed vanities carelessly and recklessly, revealing the ugly parts of mine to gain other's trust in the process. Even when I made 'exceptions' for individuals who would not suffer the wrath of my deception or glib, they were there to experience me that way. I sought my refuge in relation with other wretched people. I gave half-truths that made those listening to me encourage me when if they had known the entirety of the situation, would have run away or encouraged me otherwise. I thought this is what socializing was. I chased after depraved images and aimed at outright violations of the expectations others had for me. Whenever I returned to my beloved, a smaller man visited every time. I became the cause of my own suffering. By destroying my most intimate relationships, educational opportunities, and economic stability, I was cast into a descent. In it, I met my demons. What they told me was I was there because I had done unto another what I would not have done unto myself. I offer that to you.

I broke hearts. I hurt the people I loved. I set expectations that I failed to materialize and I did that over and over and over again. Lies are not love and deep in my Heart I knew. How could I ever utter the golden words when I was bringing the implications of my actions to the table? How could I have expected to have been tolerated by anyone when acting like that? How could I decry anything defamatory against anyone who got out of the way of such madness? And before I finally lost that trust, even with chances to recuperate, I did nothing except disappoint. Blindly, I went back on my word repeatedly and fought to maintain the power dynamics I was too blind to see were already lost. The more I consumed, the more freedom I thought I partook in. But with each complaint, conspiracy, and word, I wrapped myself in a world that was unlike anything I could have ever imagined. A nightmare, I might even say. There are periods in this life where it is difficult to get up, through, and over them.

Through addiction to substances and symbolisms, I disappointed, stagnated, and descended. I almost destroyed myself. I missed deadlines, lazily rejected earning opportunities, mismanaged my money, and spent way too much on my vices. I would not align my finances to meet the word I would put forth. I failed to equate the love I received and brutally accepted the most kindred of gifts with a soiled heart that made me unable to reciprocate. I wasted what I earned on things that did not deserve me when I should have given them to those who were. I lost many things. Hell, I gave them away. In order to see myself in the full light and darkness of my action, I had to be able to see from the exterior. In order to heal, I had to first take the sand from my eyes. That only came when I was banished from the fronts of my prospects. I was banished from my Eden. My light began to dawn only until I realized my own darkness, only when I found my dreams far away from me for the first time. Only when my acquaintances distanced themselves, only when I had no bed to sleep on, only upon leading without a love, upon betraying my goals did I ever reach this external space. Only then did the sand come off.

When the fullness of my sin came to face me, I paced miles in my one bedroom apartment. I endured great grief in this space. I relied heavily on faith to get by and with one little miracle at a time, met strangers who provided wisdom and generosity. I found timely encounters that provided food and quelled my hunger. I often had no idea where my next meal would come from. I saw I had to pass through the fire of consequence to reach the purgatory of perspective. Tears, anxiety, fear, and trembling dominated my days. I kept connecting my actions together. I accepted my situation. I did not quit. I was tempted heavily to do so. I just wrote and lived. With each memory, I recalled all of my words. I realized how easily I put myself in situations where I'd be tempted. I realized how vulnerable I was the whole time. I would confidently go in with illusions of strength and was the one who would lose. I merely enslaved myself to the line of reasoning I led proudly into the trouble with. I was the one who proudly bragged of succeeding in the arenas I now regretted. I came to fall out of love with the lifestyle I chose. The life I idealized, the one I really wanted and thought I had, which I really had only for a quarter of the time I thought I did, was gone. I saw I had it and disassembled it. I made this new bed. I had to sleep in it as long as the night was set to last. Each piece of goodness was restored as I learned to notice where it was lacking. If I was to reintegrate goodness in a domain or arena, I had to realize how wrong I was in each transgression, in each instance of reminiscence, each thought pattern. I had to see where the trouble started in the first place. It was me. Here I began to really get the chance to learn of myself. I saw how I came to behave the way I did, why I sought money and material validation to soothe an inflamed wound older than my mind could even remember, how I lost my livelihood.

When I asked my best mate how I could've traded school, a good job, a sweetheart, and stability for delinquency, he joked that it was because I was poor. But in every good joke, there is an ode to truth. Through addiction, I made myself incredibly vulnerable to desire and I now owned a heavily weakened will. Thoughts ruled me. As I uncovered the complexes that had been plaguing me since childhood, the "freedom" I thought I was partaking in with consumption resembled an escape more and more. With each discovery, I began to see myself as a scared, insecure, and desperate boy just waiting to be validated with a 'good job'. I started to see the trap. The more I soothed myself, the more I needed each day to maintain that same level of comfort. Any less comfort than yesterday was uncomfortable and chasing great euphoria meant I was uncomfortable anytime I was not on top of that hill. I saw the more I dedicated to these parts that disharmonized me, the more the call to goodness left me. I negated the loveliest things in my life for the most empty, somber, and endless desires. I realized that I felt I didn't deserve the love. With these thoughts, I reached tears. Through tears, we unleash profound things. Through sobs, the reality of the past and its lost potential were etched into my perception and being. I was humbled.

I had become the man I chose to be. With time, more and more negative adjectives could be ascribed to me by my actions. And the more I learned, the less I could hide. The less I could justify myself, I could no longer lie and say I did not have enough foresight. I couldn't bullshit myself anymore. I fought to keep the truth contained in my deceptive containers but it seeped out. If there were two signs with two arrows facing opposite directions with clear letterings of their destinations, I basically drove in the wrong direction every time. I suffered the consequences of my actions many, many times. But the lesson never sunk in. I faced the social wall and violated that. I faced the legal wall and went through that, too. I faced the personal wall and I drove right through that. Interpersonal walls? Forget about it. I could have maybe swallowed it if it had all landed on me, but it morphed the hearts of others and unnecessarily added suffering to the course of their lives. For that, I am extremely sorry. I do wince at the man that acted so callously. I was filled with a fire that burned in circles in my chest that called me closer to the truth. I recall asking, "what is this nausea I feel in my chest?" It took grit, but I accepted every ugly truth. What I wanted in those moments I regretted, I did actually want. I did partake. Each damned instance of my shortcoming would bite me and I looked with pity on the me that believed I had superseded my weakness, but was falling for it obviously.

The greatest persuasions I ever performed were not based on awards or in the esteem of the individuals I tricked, but the blasphemies I told myself. Some idiocy took me to the cold streets to wander and look for a completion that was right where I had just been. I negated the warmest sheets, the sweetest scent, care and precious kisses, a plan for the future, a good today, for cold streets. The blasphemies came to infect my ambitions. I missed deadlines I planned for and spoke of, but never did anything about. I could never share in the excitement of my peers. My inaction shined like a laser in the eye. In thought and anxiety, I would think of my brothers who were far away. Even there, I didn't call. I was often too intoxicated to do so. Vain were my days, seeking validation and position while entertaining the company in the hierarchies of other vain men. One can hear the wrestling that occurs in men's minds with the intonation, content, and delivery of his speeches. I felt them in mine. If it is a sensitive subject, you can feel the emotionality develop. You can even see the affectual manifestation of pain. This is where I came to source a lot of my understanding of what I think is right. You can see the relief and contentment of the relief when that trapped thought finally finds an outlet. We use words as far mentally as to reach for a lost sense. They veer our attention to mental imagery, swaying us to plans, daydreams, or words we think will make us more comfortable, draping reality with the lead to soothing comforts. Sadly, this effort is often futile. When it comes to what is within, there is no dollar that can buy one's Truth or a facilitative relationship with it. There is nowhere to run when one lacks it and one knows it. One's best hope is distraction.

When lack begins to be perceived in the mind, it reaches to what it feels will fill that empty feeling. In trying to avoid the anxiety that comes with freedom, one may prefer the insurance of security. One may be avoiding a task one knows is necessary or proper. The avoidance, too, is an attempt to prolong this long-coveted wholeness. While we may use words to avoid situations, they grant us access to places in our headspace. They have the power to liberate an individual actively seeking wholeness. Whether ruled by a person, or a memory, or a way of life, we have the power to change and cancel the shackles. We topple the governments in our heads because the 'people' in our thoughts simply will not take anymore. The neurons are 'fried'. We've 'had enough'. Even if it brings hunger and chaos, people would rather take that than continue being subservient to some king that is sucking the life out of life and the nation. Our attempts to change and our actualization of that change remain the revolutions of our lifetimes. These milestones are pinnacles in personality development, a triumph that yields great strength as we find the courage to overcome a complex. We 'choose' ourselves. Love drives out the hate. The masses say 'enough is enough'. The king falls.

When we deliver our speeches or voice our demands, the order our psyche yearns for is what calls out. Order demands to be re-introduced, or introduced, to a compromised value system. But to see this change through, the content of one's desires must be carefully analyzed. It is not helpful to drown people's psyches with impulsivity and intrusion, especially not our own. The urge to speak may be drawn out of some pool we have no conscious understanding of. One may be trying to go somewhere they have no conscious idea they longed for. If one does not approach their speech and the speech of others with careful consideration of one's state of mind, it will likely not reach anywhere. I don't believe we really talk 'out of our ass'. I do not believe these moments are meaningless just because we were ignorant to the deliberation going into it. These are the frequently emotional, seemingly irrational but sometimes calculated expressions of the unconscious and its repressed desires on display in real time.

One can unintentionally, intentionally, and maliciously elect what parts of the unconscious they are willing to offer someone. Young lovers say a lot when they're excited and insecure. When we flirt, it shows. In the workplace, someone's unexplored psyche could lead to them having a problem with your success. That person's perception of your success is affected by unconscious tension that has yet to be resolved within them. Another example are couples where one partner suffers addiction. They tend to be very unhappy. The addicted partner is too often preoccupied with inhabiting states of consciousness that profoundly inhibit the ability for them to relate. We save our worst words for when we are most afraid or angry. More malicious expressions of unconscious resentment manifest in those passive aggressive comments or in those implicit accusations. Without an understanding of our internalities, these cruelties will simply fly right by us and remain common practice.

In all these examples, the speaker is doing something fascinating. The speaker is fending off abstract threats with an abstract form of violence. The primitivity is still dominating but it appears as though it were from a different but co-existing dimension. In an argument, it almost seems like humans 'bark' at each other. We just recognize the sound of those barks and we call it speech. While most do not bite (I knew someone once who did), we attack with the cognitive abilities we do have. The individual weaponizes their cognition in order to provoke a reaction that would entail a desired change. These expressions form, maintain, and epitomize a mental structure we conceptualize called comfort. The harms of violating this desired state are clear. We consider an avoidance of this violation civil. We share this understanding to avoid hurting one another directly. Instead of violence, we elicit change this way, with rules and expectations. But because others cannot explicitly read our minds, we conjure expressions for change in a million different ways. Not only do we use words to protect ourselves this way, but we use them to gain strategic advantages. Deception occurs in the sensitive transfer of information and the strategic distortion of our language.

When one is lied to, a flurry of emotions ensues. The reality that one was deemed not worthy enough to hear the truth arises. The individual will inevitably wonder what it was about themselves that caused the rejection or distortion of information. Thoughts run. Were the deceived expected to fumble the truth? Was that it? Paranoia and suspicious thinking come to infect the psyche. What was the reason for the exclusion? When I imagined the ones I loved most being those I lied to most boldly, my empathetic sense broadened. The more I investigated my foolery, the more allergic I became to its manifestation. Philosophy began to change for me, conversation did, too, even the way I walked. I came to see myself as the biggest hypocrite for how great were the towers of my rhetoric and how empty was every room. I made fools of those that cared about me most. A person's integral structure crumbles a bit more with every little lie. The deceived can come to question their own ability to tell reality and illusion apart, unwilling to relinquish the trust they are dependent on. They question whether they might be the liars. We fall into the trap. We get persuaded and deceived.

I see a world of idols today in our society that runs rampant with persuasion and deception. It is of dire concern to me now because I felt one soul ravaged by the pushes and pulls of a 'demonic' incentive. I dislike imagining a world full of it. Today, one does not have to look far to feel the tugs of persuasion and deception. They are present in our governments, celebrities, advertisements, newspapers, and media outlets. They sell our identities, bombard us with things to indulge our senses, reducing the passion that comes with struggling for them. The feeling comes to be regarded equally as the effect. We can be seduced to live according to this indulgence. The lifestyles of the addicted and the insane reflect this. Persuasion and deception paints the picture before we even know there is a canvas. We make enemies as we heed other's grievances. Propaganda plays this game. We can grow skeptical of other's intentions because of an experience or what we have heard. That skepticism could prevent the benefit of the doubt, it often does. Then, from the high levels of politics to the level of the household, bitter rivalries are at risk of breaking out. Trust is lost. War is likely. When the hope of viable and consistent is lost, contact among the individuals is usually broken. Here, the great nation states come out and so do divorced couples. Often, they wonder how the old team or a pair of old friends fell apart.

If one reads about history, the pattern is clear. The concealment, distortion, restriction, and exaggeration of truth raises hell. It took me a long time to realize it but it is quite simple. We rely on an intelligible and consistent delivery of accurate and realistic recollections. Insofar as we align ourselves with truth, we will gain the respect and trust of others. Today, truth gets woefully neglected. We care more for the aesthetic of it all. Contempt is thrown at the truth's excavation. It has been reduced to interpretation. We live in a culture that considers it successful to deceive successfully. How should we expect to continue on with the potency of our nuclear weapons without a commitment to earnest relations? How are we supposed to discipline ourselves without 'meaning'? In a hyper-organized society like ours where violations of the social contract are easier than ever before, what is it going to take? We must know the Self. It wouldn't hurt to love it, either. But if one cannot achieve such a thing, one must face the questions internally that answer the question of why the Self is not accessible. If we don't come to this self-love, I think we risk the potential inside of us and the beautiful moments that come from that potential's materialization. Why do we negate the chance to love ourselves? Why do we become like those who hurt us? Why blame others when we are patiently waiting for an opportunity to return that very same wrong?

I heard once that all warfare was based on deception. And when I think about how trust is made and broken, how crime grows in a group, how corruption is normalized, and war deemed inevitable, all I see are the stirrings and clashings of Man's Hearts. The delusions that shadow its beauty are apparent in dramatic death counts. So when I see the damage I did to my livelihood and those of other people, I am compelled, dragged by the chain of atonement to write this. If one can learn to see where these idols are enforced and reinforced, where persuasion keeps trapping us, and where the deception may be blinding us, then maybe we can keep ourselves alive, make ourselves 'better', and keep the love in our relationships intact. Maybe then, we can keep the nuclear bombs from being set off. For those of us who have fit into the shoes of malady and evil and walked in them, the commitment to that 'better' is only the beginning of one's atonement. Only then can the fight begin. One must swear by a commitment to never walk *that* way again. A weak person can say they have lied and a strong one can seek forgiveness in their confession, but powerful indeed are those who are committed to never lying again. When one hoards the truth from someone, one has stopped the flow of objective reality from flowing through the psyches of those involved. The path of truth is obstructed not by Truth's demands but by our fears.

As long as deception remains, the Heart will continue on the deceptive cycle as it attempts to recover from each previous deception. The poison becomes the medicine and so it goes, on and on. After enough lies, the wall deception builds can grow thick enough that one may no longer hear the whisperings of another's Heart. Moments like these are disastrous in matters of foreign policy and torturous in the matters of love. Seneca, anyone? With lies, we grow apart. With each one, the wall grows a little taller and a little thicker. This metaphorical wall is really the distance the ego perceives between self and another. The ability to relate, the foundation of love, becomes weakened. It requires more and more effort. Employing deception due to the unwillingness to accept reality, one may justify one's methodology for the sake of self-comfort. Each lie we tell ourselves is like a bruise to our relationship with reality. In regards to another, it diminishes a crucial trust. Remember that a lie must be told to oneself first before it can be projected onto another. We have to run it by our reason to ascertain its viability, which is its believability. With compulsive liars, lying becomes systematic and can be conceived with remarkable versatility and verbal flexibility. From one bullshitter to another, the most dangerous of liars are not those that lie most frequently, but those that remain committed to remaining hidden amongst truth-sayers. Due to differing necessities among the masses, conflict will come, but deception, my friends, is what will cause conflict to be our demise.

We are at this point as a globe. We don't even trust each other enough, but we do not ourselves trustworthy enough either. We assign blame to those who are suspicious of us as if we have been totally available and eager for dialogue and reason. Persuasion and deception runs off the schemas in our head. We will inevitably approach people with the conceptions we have of them, often reducing the connection in the interaction between those persons. If we lie and reinforce the lie of its worth to us, then we have a problem. If we cannot let it go, it has us. I've heard the phenomena of this being called 'encapsulation' or 'obsession' when it becomes very persistent. People do it with drugs, other people, jobs, and group identities. It is all out of the fact that a number of people find trust to be a very hard thing to find. And when they believe they have found it, or they have deluded themselves with distortions or exaggerations about it, they run to strange ends to keep them logically viable. We may have the habit of projecting habitually, idolizing ritualistically, and engaging religiously with some of these bonds.

The more frequently one is lied to, the easier it becomes for that person to lie. The tactic is learned as it is suffered. The advantage is seen by the novice and used at a later time. We've been doing it for a long time, too. We've been on that since we got smart. The problem is, most of our wars, internal and external, are rooted in deception. By adopting the practice of lying, one feels a sense of liberation from the suffering, but that is the same course of action the one who deceived them employed. One first believes lying prevents the damage being lied to would cause. In order to mitigate deception, however, one must learn why one does it in the first place. It is not hard to see just how great of a disadvantage we stand at in this world if we continue this damned malpractice. From the truth's withered bark burns the fire that sheaths the divisive sword of the lie. The fluidity of truth, like a pitcher of water, finds lies like sand. Enough of it, and the sand will absorb the truth and one will forget water ever took its place. The trust is gone, love leaves. At this point, if one were to launch a hostile attack of any kind, things are likely to get ugly. This happens in foreign policy and interpersonal relationships alike. The need to return the damage, equalize it, and combat it with an equally sufferable form characterizes the state of war.

Enslavement is the result of deception, for one attaches and commits oneself to a fragile web of lies. One acts often out of 'duty' to one's conceptions. War is no different. Entire societies of millions could be gobbled up by the ideologies and pockets of a few hundred, or a couple thousands. We cannot allow ourselves to get there, and when there we must get out. The enslavement begins in the Mind and will forever exist only in the Mind. The tortured are led by an 'order' they understand to torture others, often by the same methods they were tortured. The enslaved and the slave holder will remain experiencing life in an almost second-hand style, as though maintaining the bond were the best life has to offer.

My agency came to be the wall that prevented the flow of other's truth. This was my greatest transgression. I enslaved and was enslaved. I impeded instead of encouraged. I judged instead of understood. I regarded before respecting. I spoke so as to be heard without a care for being understood. I had an affair with my intellect. I chased after her objects and in lust wasted my evenings. I found myself in the passion of those figures and mannerisms of which I lusted for and passed into the night restless and unsatisfied. I made the mistake of being ungrateful for the day by coveting the privacy of the night. A remorseful and repentant heart offers you its confession. By the tremor of my hands, smile lost in time, and the trickle of hope in my sight, I recognize that I have sinned, deceiver, and felt loss by my own hands and short-sightedness. I promoted what I preached against and I have done wrong. My sandcastles have been washed along the shores of Truth. I came to be a king of nothing and understandably, my 'subjects' left the shitstorm that was, after all, only a sandcastle. I was the government that was toppled. Once the charmer oozing righteous rebellion, I was one of the revolutionaries who became the dictator. I lived and felt the coup d'etat. I have seen my statues destroyed and my gods replaced. I no longer crave power, only freedom. I crave not a web of lies, nor the pond of my comfort, but a deep swim in Her sea.

    I struggle with seeing the strategic nature of advertisement, pinning our primitive proclivities against us. When commerce begins to go beyond ethical constraints and starts to bend the truth, we shouldn't start to question what deception is and what it isn't. We know what it is. I am wary of the force deception exerts in this world because I have seen, felt, and suffered its consequences. And as long as the nuclear warheads remain pointed at each other, I think we all ought to be a bit concerned, too. If we are on the path of the Self, we cannot follow or walk the path of any other. Without the commitment to honesty, how should we conduct our diplomatic endeavors? I am not one to prioritze a certain way to walk. If I did, I believe I stand as arrogant, but I do advocate for a world that pleads with others to remember what matters. I do advocate and plead for at least a minimal inspection of the urgings swaying our psyches. The urgings tell of the contents of one's Heart. I urge one to scale that mountain. I urge against the cowardice of deception, arguing there is much greater courage in acceptance and care. One does not have to destroy everything to learn how dangerous deception can be. I did and that is why I write.

The respects we pay, the direction of our cares, the attention we dedicate all tell of our idols. It is not so much that our idols are 'wrong', but that they tell more of what is in us. If we agree with certain individuals that represent certain values, then the values are shared. Only when two individuals reach an agreement is there a union. A human who craves union will often take any union, but that union could may well be an agreement on different pretenses. The parties involved could be getting different things. This is a transactional bond not a substantial one. Compatibility does not make anything superior or healthy, it just means the properties blend together or find use in each other. Our beliefs have not proven sufficient in preventing malady. So today, as we face mass media, mass advertisement, mass commercialization, mass government, racism, and political totalism, we cannot just float each day by. We cannot act according to the way things are presented to us. We cannot complacently take deception. Our Hearts grow bitter when we do that and the debate on values grows increasingly scrutinized. Nothing is a good enough reason to abandon yourself unless a greater you awaits you on the other side.

The dizziness of today's society has made the "values" of yesterday easily disregardable. We live in a time that hates tradition. As tradition which is the collection of habits rooted in observations and wisdom far before our time gets done away with, a recrudescence to replace its order manifests. Just as in the case when a new government absorbs the power vacuum left behind by an old government. The 21st century is only the beginning of the next chapter of our development. It is characterized by its incredible capacity to persuade masses and instill deception without its persons even knowing. These mediums transfer persuasion and deception easier than ever before. And as this reality is becoming increasingly capitalized and its malevolence ever more apparent, I think we need to open our eyes. If we are to avoid the recurrence of the genocides, we must heed ourselves first. We must peer into why we succumb to dictators in matters of politics and the Heart. What leads us to lie to our spouses? Why do we give up our livelihoods for the neverland in our heads? Why are we unfaithful to the truths of our Hearts? And if so, why do we choose to enter a nature we often detest in order to avoid it, getting even further from what it asks of us? Why don't we see it until we are far from who we were?

    In our day and age, I think the problem is that we actually believe our lies. In the twenty-first century, our architectural sights, our unquestioned access to simple necessities, and multitudes of entertainment services, make our lies easy to believe. We glorify them. We dramatize them for our entertainment. We implement that drama into our lives to make ourselves relevant. We conjure our approaches like snakes in the grass. We centralize the factors to meet the demands our desires require, often for attention, frequently out of jealousy. All this seems to stem from the fact that we live isolated. We struggle in the rich world with the idea of community. Because comfort has become so prioritized, we live estranged from a part of our nature that is only revealed in times of suffering. As a result, we avoid it. Plain and simple. Too often, we may be afraid of the pain the truth is likely to cause. We may avoid the chaos the truth within may provoke because then we must see who has been lying and learning of being deceived is one of the most painful psychic experiences one can go through. Trauma can result when an individual is exposed to betrayal repeatedly. I offer you this insight into what happens when we lie to ourselves for too long.

In order to grow resilient against the persuasion and deception, we must grow wary of what others call the truth. We must be even more wary of what we feel confirms our truth, what we call evidence in relation the function of belief. We live with this silly idea that the more something is agreed with, the truer it is. We often point to the crowd's adherence to a cause or a claim as testimony to its validity. We also have a tendency to actively seek out information that correlates with and confirms our thinking. And even when one manages to evade the temptation of group thinking, one still has to speak the language of the crowd in order to even get by. The quickest way to make enemies in a group is to espouse a belief that goes against the grain of what they think is true. We may believe something the crowd does not like or may see identify a task that hasn't been done or something they are not willing to admit they have done or the hypocrisy in the accusations they throw or the innocence of those they hide behind. Those who identify these markers of failure in a group are those who have found the rudiments of what it means to lead. We believe things exist the way we'd like to think about them. We align our thoughts with the designations society has given to things and gear our goals to the destinations of its promises and our opinions about nearly everything fall victim to this tendency. To be one's own requires one to be strong.

One of my mother's phrases was 'make a reputation and go to sleep." To me, it reinforced the notion of the relentlessness of opinion. Opinions are limited in their defining power, but they sure have a way of influencing other opinions. The adjectives we associate with experiences don't determine an object's nature, they tell more of the pedagogical influence the object had on the experiencer. If an experience was unpleasant, the adjective likely to be associated with will be negative. We will call it 'bad' or some adjective along the line. If one calls a situation crazy, one is describing a condition where there was no apparent 'rationale' the experiencer could see. As people, we naturally use information from the outside world. Many judgments are made by what one hears about what or how things were. Words, again, are limited. We weren't there. We didn't feel it. Hearing a trusted opinion is often sufficient enough to sway another. This is due to the power of trust where the trusted's opinion is taken as Truth in the listener's Heart. Someone's bad experience may have been better expressed with more accurate terminology. Most probably, a more accurate assessment would have been 'I do not wish to repeat that', instead of declaring something of poor quality as 'futile'.

Negative recountings and pessimistic references are not a determination of anything's nature other than the speaker's standing relations with whatever is being mentioned. Every description is a story. If one really listens, one can even imagine the experience of the speaker by hearing the emotion conveyed in a recollection. You can even imagine the direction the speaker's fight or flight response took in their recounting without them even telling you, but they don't tell the whole story. Commonly, descriptions are taken as warnings to avoid hazards. Anthropologically, this makes great sense. But great delusions can manifest as a result of those same instinctual safeguards. Simply put, we can be wrong. We can conjure danger about people and things that actually don't have much harm in them. The same occurs with positive descriptions, just the other way around. Then, impressions fly and as powerful as I mentioned groupthinking to be, we may want to remain in the group and carry on with what someone thinks about something. Receiving a consistent negative opinion from someone very close to us can leave a dramatic effect on the qualitative direction of our own opinion. Something is not the word that is used to describe it. Remember this, my friends. A word is a word, but a thing is a thing and something is its own thing. Whatever it is, it is definitely not the word. We should not be persuaded a way with words without heeding the circumstances, biases, motives, and prejudices of the speaker carefully.

Because words have their limits, almost everything we say is a distortion of truth. This is partially why some Buddhist monks take oaths of silence. It does not mean we are malicious, it is simply that reality cannot be explained in totality. This is why we call people effective at describing things as articulate. Persuasion and deception is not as simple as an absolute blanket to drape over that or this. That doesn't mean we have to stop talking. I am not saying we should throw out words. They have their place. Like in the case of a country, it has a name and defined borders, but the name of the country does not attest to the substance of the soil. The animals don't know the difference. Even though some can come to identify strongly with their nation, the name of a country remains merely a marker of reference for something's appreciated history. Titles and ranks and names get transformed into an end in the minds of men. When we start to believe this country is 'superior' to that country, now we are fighting with ideas that have no actual basis in substance. Comparison cannot achieve an end by the methodology it seeks. To compare things is often foolery and yet it takes up the great portion what the masses talk about. Identification with things one is not is a subtle sign of trouble.

Most people are persuaded through small talk. It offers the opportunity bring our cognitive tools together as a team. We try to capture the nature of objective reality with our subjectively relative toolsets. We throw out words and emotions and indulge in the sentiments those words and emotions produce in us. It can be very amusing, but maintaining the positive emotions of small talk often takes the forefront of the discussion. For this reason, we very often only achieve emotionality and vanity in debate. We do not argue to collectively win, we instead play on the side of our beliefs with the intent to defend them. This way, we can actually grow more at odds with the truth as we try to nail it down. Words too often merely inflame us and put us in a state of fighting, fawning, fleeing, or freezing, making it crucial this to detach from the emotions words produce. This way, we can see things a little differently. Maybe then, the tyrant is no longer a god decrying our worth, instead a vain and small man trying to make himself feel better by implementing childhood coping mechanisms. This helps with social anxiety. Once we can see ourselves without our vanity, the power of our delusions and exaggerations begins to fade. One's ability to resist persuasion grows and one becomes immensely cognizant of the ubiquitousness of deception. One's rationale grows as does one's sense. Willpower then grows too. Others' ideas become silly when one is no longer attached to their definitions in the mind.

Things cannot be substantially altered or objectively a way just by our say. A declaration of something does not change its actual nature or chemical structure, it can only alter the attitude a perciever takes to reality. Lying, however, attempts to do just this. Lying incurs delusion in another as a means of hiding from the consequences of reality. It is inherently arrogant and self-centered behavior. We attempt to immobilize another's agency by overwhelming their intuition through the freezing their senses so to not see them act a certain way. When manic, we can put ourselves out there so drastically while hiding so cleverly and sinisterly to keep our resources and reputation intact. The one being deceived may be so encapsulated by the speaker that the speaker's approval rules over the listener's emotional states. Some people live through words this way. I find it an an exhausting and debasing way to live. When another is the director of our temperaments, we have the most dangerous form of idolatry. To depend on one's approval is a sign of deep attachment and it inherently undermines self-worth. It is a sign of a profound desire of some kind and the urge to control tells more of the controller than the controlled in terms of what is wrong. It is sufferable for all involved. Even the dominant players in this dynamic life run pained and confused, prompting and inspiring fear and trembling anytime they feel their web of lies are threatened, maybe this has happened to you.

For individuals obsessed with controlling and the controlled, great complexes hide behind their behaviors. Their insecurities are like beasts that lurk in their psychic blind spots. For the disturbed, the sensation of isolation, of perceived abandonment, of becoming the 'best', or being 'left' quickly form snowballs that grow as they roll down the thoughts of these poor individuals. This happens to everyone but in some it is a constant occurrence. It is a hallmark feature of the borderline personalities. Without intervention, expression, or social contact, the brain's neural circuit can come to be affected by these a lot. The ball grows with each perceived association, each memory ballooning the fantasy one escapes to in order to deal with the threat in mind. We may grow evermore frightened, hateful, or prejudiced because of the words we're using in our mind. This way, our perception gets far from our bodies by relying too much on our words.

Deception critically inhibits the progression and growth of society. It dissolves individuals' ability to make proper decisions as they receive inaccurate assessments, resulting in misguided assessments. The deceived are isolated to a unique and misconstrued perception molded by the deceiver. They often lose the trust of the social groups they travel through. With persuasion and deception, we get access to a temporary but very dangerous advantage. We distort another's understanding of reality in order to buy some time. With a lie, you buy time. Whether it is the false promise or the justification regarding one's shortcoming, one arrogantly assumes they can soften the impact of a failure with a rationale for their course of action. Not only is it a failure to achieve, but it is also a failure to accept the consequences of one's failure. It breaks the state of responsibility. It is a weakness on the part of the individual to face the reality pertinent to them. People pay for being irresponsible. Many think the excuse is the answer, the complaint the remedy. Some of us are so unwilling to face the reality that is concurrent with our actions one retreats into a persona or ideology for the rest of their lives. When one tells the truth, one is at least comfortable enough to face the reality one exists in. The weak individual, however, will desperately claw and deceive to buy enough time to conjure the next reinforcement of the original lie. Because we preserve ourselves instinctively, it tends to continue on and on until the truth is faced or it faces us. This is the liar's cycle.

  The truth fills in the limitations of our existence. The fact one cannot be two places at once prevents one from knowing the fullness of a situation, the breadth of the will other people are employing. The truth fills in these gaps. When one is left in the dark, when we lie or are lied to, we can be left alone on a conceptualized and distorted reality only the deceivers and the deceived live on. The difference of the quality of life between the two is extreme, even though both tend to be poor. In relationships, a deceptive and insecure foundation can lead to profoundly altering experiences as emotions run wild. It can be traumatic and tragic.

In interpersonal relations, one may not be willing to concede their role in this game. It entails admitting the darker side of the psyche may be driving the person. Through hopes and delusions, one may grow impaired. One may become too afraid to act a certain way. We can convince ourselves and others of the ideas we have for reality. It is often a self-serving one. We could even be blind to that. Down to the level of what we appreciate, we could be lying to ourselves about what is worthwhile and what is not. Desire, however, can disturb and even overtake one's ability to gauge risk and loss. If the individual idolizes a certain way, a ruthless attitude can be adopted for assuring the presence of the idol. People can come to disregard loss if it means the presence of their idol is assured. People convince themselves to keep on destroying what is good to avoid the fear of abandonment. Oh! The things we tell ourselves to be this foolish! Most often, these things we tell are far from the truth. I warn, my friends, that great cowardice is found in great deception. Great cruelty exists when pleasure is taken in the 'success' of a deception. A coward is the sinner who feels stronger for escaping their circumstance and letting the pain pass on to another. When one cannot trust, one will lie. One will lie to oneself. Unable to commit to oneself, one will, ultimately, be unable to commit to others. I suffered from this. I loved selfishly which is to say my love went no direction at all.

I lied because I was afraid to lose and though I longed for my beloved and times past, who can trust a liar?

The distrustful person swears by the potential harm that one's inattention can attract, but I offer a thought. What about the good we can miss? You'll never know how much you are loved. I only got an idea until I could no longer access that love from certain someones that were my world. You'll never have the full range of the inaccuracy of your opinions. I realized this when the warmest eyes grew cold and a few unions I were far gone. I do not wish this experience on another. Many of us have experienced the force of the world's temptations. And like clockwork, a great skepticism has run across our cultures. Skepticism is the only natural response to a world full of idols. With more information than ever before, it is no surprise we have forgotten that great tyrants and oppressive systems have fallen by the grace a few brave and heroic skeptics. So we must ask, in this age of advertisement, commercialism, legalism, and materialized values, to what extent should we believe the claims made by a product's marketer? To what extent can we consider their regulation? Their regulators? The validity of the regulator? What about how they are regulated? We must be able to answer why they should be regulated and what the limits of those regulators should be? How much should I believe and how should I believe it? These are all valid thought streams worth digging into when one has the time. A great disheartening occurs when the motivations that push the self become visible. Do not grow weary of them. We do not need to be suspicious of ourselves this deeply, only of the images leading us to think the way we do. Too often, the truth's tenets are ignored in this analysis and projected onto the Other or tragically repressed into the Dark.

As our responsibilities become expectations and business stacks on its initiatives in our everyday lives, our behavior runs the risk of growing farther and farther out of our hands. If individuality is diminished, then the collective takes the driver seat. We understand the reciprocal ambition of human nature. Living a life that is not according to our Truth is a lie in its own form. With our augmenting material incentives, we can sense this lack of authenticity in culture, commerce, and cinema. And in our everyday interactions, we see nothing different. Giving is not the same when it is expected. We go to work without loving the work we do. We trade mindlessly at the cash register. This society is having its way with us. We talk strategically, objectify and pragmatize, sucking everything we can out of resources to please us. All the while, we denigrate any virtue relevant to suffering, stifling the utility we can gauge out of it for the perception of what it cannot. It is all about the intention and the effect in union. This way, two could be doing the same thing but by the commitment of the Heart from which it comes, they are doing two very different things.

Under this light I close this chapter with these questions. Just because you gave something to someone, how much did you give of yourself in what you gave? If we feed a man and prolong his life, but reduce the act to a duty, what was really prolonged? In the pursuit of profit, advertisements, personal modifications, and a growing reliance on social media, are we really getting closer to a trajectory that satisfies our urgency for a meaningful life? Is it mature enough to expect it to be found in a product, a substance, or a follower count? And when we feel we have gotten closer to anything, how far have we really gotten to anything but our own idea of that thing? In a world where righteousness is equatable to agreeableness, are we seriously going to run with the crowd this way? If popularity could shift away from virtues as can the masses' preferences, should what is idolized really be the determinant of what should be? Should we engage with these idols at all? If we do, to what extent? I ask you.

In the hearts of abusers, tyrants, and toddlers, it will always be about the wants. As long as there are people who think like toddlers, there will always be adults in charge of putting them in their place. So, if one person finds success in wealth and material mediums but their Heart still whispers of something 'more', I say listen to it. It may just be that the gains in those material systems may not be the yearnings of that lost one's Heart. Don't go so far from your Heart that you become blind by the madness of this world. If consequences come to your door, open the door. If it takes you away from your beloved and old dreams, then so be it. If you have to be hated for something you think is right, right on. Really, just really consider if it is right and if you still sense that it is, don't fold. Because despite the fact our system continues to promote its harms, we have the choice to embrace those persuasions or not. We could be the star in someone's night sky by simply being ourselves. With the truth, we can spread warmth and light. We could also be that ray of sunshine that stabs the sleepy eye. With this chance to be warmth and light, we can become hope and comfort in a world of idols that leaves us all cold. We could become hope to a populace running around chasing, one that does not understand what it craves nor why it craves it.

    Be wary, my friends, of persuasion and deception. I have persuaded and deceived and suffered as a result. I can stand with all those who have been persuaded and deceived and with those who have persuaded and deceived. Either which, I urge you, my friends, to grow not bitter. Yes, people deserving of recognition are regularly neglected by nepotism, paraded by corruption, and rewarded for their incessant greed. Immense bureaucratically-managed political and commercial machines get away with profound exploitations, often without any consequences. Media companies capitalize on all of our plights, finding stories where there are none and making others where they want one. Actual happenings get extended to unreasonable limits in the attempt to sway people's attention from their intuitive truths to artificial pursuits, all for the sake of profit. The persuaders and deceivers poke and toy at the inflammatory part of our psyches in the attempt to veer us to their hopes. We must be wary of the internal predispositions, intentions, and philosophies of those commandeering our institutions of work, education, and governance. They too, in all their material and titular glory, remain susceptible to the primitivity frequently forgotten by the prestige of their institutes. The adoration of their symbols and the mask of civility does not change their limits. We are subject to them too After all, everyone needs a restroom.

The Heart will always seek to be in line with its truth. The lives we lead today may lead us to feel the ravenous torment of choosing our loyalties, but I urge you, my friend, to fear not. Never let your own thoughts fool you. I say this with the most cathartic heart I can: don't lie to anyone, nor to yourself. Don't overestimate what is behind you and don't leave your best self on the shelf. Remember the more you want is the less you have. Don't stay when you are not valued and do not force what is not wanted. Don't forget what you've learned. The mitigation of risk begins with prevention. It is infinitely greater to learn, not repeat, and do than learn, preach, and never act. I lived as the vain preacher and came out as a representative for hypocrisy. Remember to never fear when you are banished, you can remake yourself. Making a friend of truth will make you a friend of many. I urge you to control the story you tell yourself. Be like a tree, nice and straight, because no amount of charisma, vocabulary, or flattery can match the aged and consistent taste of authenticity. The lesson I share here is that the Heart seeks truth and men who do not care for it alienate the righteous by their own hand.

The Heart will not forgive us for our weakness and it will restore the order it sees fit. Life naturally brings us to these monumental moments. So when those judgment days come, what will you choose? When the universe brings you to the moment of decision, how many times will you reject your pedigree and pick the degeneracy? Are we supposed to live these lies our entire lives? Will our fears keep determining our direction, our tears speaking for us? Or can we take our fear away from the chase for control, comfort, and direct it to the awesome force of the Truth. Could we perhaps respect the fact of our very existence and face the reality for what it is worth and maybe even bear it with some grace? We cannot keep lies up forever because so awesome is the force of Truth that its gravity inevitably pulls every lie apart. So who here is bold enough to face their loneliest loneliness and meet their nature? Who will use that knowledge not to gain advantage over his fellow man, but to become better able to serve him? Will we choose the vain conception or finally take our special role as one among the many parts? Shall we continue to cower as false kings, fooled by our long procrastinated 'start'? Or will we pay homage and finally take that trip into those pesky and elusive susceptibilities of the Heart?

IV

Susceptibilities of the Heart

Few but great are the susceptibilities of the Heart. A generation with no Heart knows little of them, yet is greatly moved by them. Thought can construct these great structures in the Mind about others and the self but no self-knowledge is possible without the credence the Heart demands. It really is something to get to know your own Heart. Many reduce the Heart to a metaphor, a brain, a label, a 'knowing' of sorts. These word lovers deem themselves wise, persuading the many with their comports. A generation like this is one without Heart. Its people know no love, only longing. There are not enough willing to reciprocate love. A generation with no love knows nothing but wanting. Desire gets toyed with but its roots get no attention. The Heart is the bridge between the external and the internal where Nature and God sow the fabric of one's very own essence. The Heart is what makes us unique in our relation to all Being. But in this world, it is too often silenced by the pains of the past, by loves that had to part. One stifles oneself with doubts. One only needs to realize that only the Mind can blind a Heart to a Being that never comes apart.

The world has this way of influencing the Mind.

Consequently, the Heart rarely gets its way in this world. People rarely end up in places they once hoped for. In fact, we frequently find ourselves in places that we never imagined. It is because of worldly demands the Heart gets pulled away from one way and towards another. Out of insecurity, decisions are made to restore security and when others offer their opinions about the decisions taken to restore that order and more decisions end up being made in response to the effect of those opinions. Inevitably, we react. Some of these decisions pull us away from what we are striving for, the urge to address consequences can replace or supersede our desires. Often, it leaves outcomes we didn't ask for. The Heart may be torn by the love of another or a duty the Mind has convinced itself is worth bearing. The Heart may struggle with accommodating the order and rationale of the Mind. It could very well be the other way around. The body perceives differently than the Mind. The Mind may not be willing to accept the desires of one's Heart, especially if those desires conflict with some social expectation or the education one has received. When one is taught and convinced their needs cannot be met under certain conditions, it will tend to avoid those conditions even it is the Heart that longs to be there. The Mind must convince itself over and over that the conditions away from the Heart's wants are satisfactory. A person who has not realized their Heart or lives neglecting it suffers this way.

  The seat of the Person is The Heart. It is the nucleus of our psyche, the root of our identity, and the resultant the 'good' in every person. The Heart naturally covets and longs. In tandem with Nature, it is the servicer of our needs, the wellspring of all emotion, and consequently the pipeline to the Soul. The Heart cannot be touched, but as long as one is alive and breathing, it is always sensed. It is the funnel that personifies sense, the complot of a human personality. The

Heart is uniquely present in one's relationship with Life as a whole. It is the center of all personified organization. It can be disoriented, empowered, and solidified. Yet, we most commonly come to recognize its presence and purpose when it is damaged. What the Heart is is tied to the body. It remains, however, ultimately independent of it. The body seeks its reproduction and preservation and our thoughts follow the same accord. The Mind often suggests a destination and to the Body a state on which to embark to achieve this end This occurs most often by suggesting a certain avenue of action or directing one to a certain action. This is where the Mind and Heart most frequently conflict, the cases when the Heart fights the rationale of the Mind. The Heart is the bridge where the Totality of Nature meets the subtle nuances of our genetics, situations, and decisions to give us a situation we call our own. In these longings, it seeks to make us 'whole'. It longs to make us One, even when 'wrong'.

    The Heart is the seat of all perception, the point from which all things within emerge. It stands to receive and it is in place to give. Depending on what one has received and what one has given, the Mind finds itself with numerous quirks to want certain things in certain ways and at certain times. These quirks come to form the Personality which despite being largely inherited is made unique by the experiences, choices, and times one is subject to. Much of what the Heart receives cannot be remembered for its memory is not limited to Mind. It is the Body as much as the Mind. The Body and Mind may work in tandem to keep one alive, but the Heart is the powerhouse that keeps each person unique. Every person longs to have their Heart recognized. It is like a glass that longs to be full. After all, it wants to serve its purpose. And when it comes to actions, it is mainly the Mind that is the actor. The world would prefer to keep it that way. Minds can be conditioned but Hearts cannot.

One's Heart includes all of one's memories and the resulting style it has incorporated for the way it believes and does. Personality and Mind function in tandem, producing methodologies for the way we know to crave, think, and express ourselves. We pick up on things we appreciate, from what stuns us, from what feels good, from what we have seen as effective. These appreciations emerge from the Body's understanding to thrive. These methodologies lead us to who we love, how we love, and the unique goals and ideals we hold that ultimately distinguish us from others. Our quirks, however, frequently run into a world that seeks predictability and uniformity. Our Hearts rarely get to express ourselves to the degree we often long for. The world wants unpredictable people they can predictably appreciate. When we are not predictable to others, the world grows unpredictable for us. It takes effort to retain a stability we like to call a livelihood, the 'world' depends on it. And even with the most appreciated and loved livelihoods, the susceptibilities of the Heart still spring up. They take us on detours without regard to our best efforts to remain 'on track'. No matter how conditioned the environment, we still grow distracted. In spite of the combination of Nature's demands, our Personality's tendencies, the Mind's complexes, our wishes, the state of our Body, the needs of the World, and the skepticism of our Hearts, desires come to the Mind and Heart.

The presence of the Heart can be observed in some form or fashion in everything we do. Because action requires effort and effort is correlated to desire, the absence of Heart can inversely be observed in everything we don't do. The amount of Heart present is often directly observed in the presence of visible effort. This 'presence' is affected heavily by what we idolize. So effort is not so simple, it is multi-faceted. In this life, the Heart struggles with Mind to ascertain what deserves effort and what does not. The Mind plans in accord with what it deems reasonable. Anyone who has loved or felt duty knows the Heart does not follow such an accord. We often call those suffering from this pendulum of a lifestyle 'conflicted'. We say their Heart is 'torn'. Or when a person is hesitant or lazy, it is assumed quickly their Heart is = 'not in it'. The world transversely has its wants for us and we have our wants from it. Naturally, they disagree. The external world cannot deliver the content of our desires in the quantities and fashion we'd like. That is as simple as that. Because of this silly little fact of life, we convince ourselves our Hearts are worth neglecting. Our efforts may end up going some other way.

     The language of the Heart is love. So known is this, most call it a motif. Love can be used here as unification, alignment, connection, or harmony. The Heart tries to hold everything about who we are together, as seen in the workings of the psyche. It longs to be connected. The Heart works with the Mind to keep our friends, livelihoods, and ambitions intact. Even the relationship we have with ourselves gets worked and maintained by the Heart. It works with the body and its systems to keep us in a place we feel is appreciable. Our truth seeks to be one with the Truth supporting its existence. Because we don't know the totality of Truth, we constantly rely on others to inform us. But instead of listening to each other's Hearts, or hearing out our own longings, we convince ourselves such an investigation is child's play in a world rampant with idols. We sacrifice the self for the group, keeping things surface level, pushing the innards down. Those who reject the opportunity to connect frequently grow cold and resentful hearts. But I have rarely found much fault with these loveless individuals who push reality away because of the fear of facing disappointment in the face of a world that rarely caters to the Heart. I, in fact, can relate. But the reality is without connection, there is no love.

     Circumstance gives some individuals' a longer road to

tread on the course of their journeys to their Heart's desires than others. This is another fact of life. Regardless, so great can one's conviction to the Heart be that some are willing to take more steps than others. Some are willing to die for what their Heart holds dear. Many call these people admirable, many call them fools. The difference between the two is whether the world thought their desires were 'reasonable' or not. Then again, the world did not possess that martyr's Heart. No one lives another's life. The world quickly, consistently, and ardently offers its opinion as though it did. The World sadly often works to keep the longings of Hearts from manifesting. This happens because of the childish longing for power. The Mind then may convince the dreamer that the calls of their Heart are not worthwhile for this reason or that reason. Heavy and burdened are these Hearts. Most drag themselves around until they reach old age simply carrying out worldly obligations, finding pleasures where possible. Many people like this continue living solely for the sake of living, surviving but never drawing. The only fight these people embark on is the fight to not want what they truly desire. Circumstance convinces some this is a worthwhile way of life.

Dark and lonely can these Hearts become. The corners of their memories are painted with the same colors of their formerly lit horizons. Lost smiles hide among those horizons. These images torment the Heart, the Mind with anxiety, manifest in the Spirit as obsession and resentment. Spirit. The inability to love what one loves is hell for the Heart. It is to be locked out of paradise. Thoughts go negative. They get heavy. The Heart weakens. The Mind begins to overtake one's internal harmony. The Mind can cause us a difficult life. When disordered, the body takes everything in stressfully. The relationship between the Body's ambitions and the Mind's tendencies bleed into one another. Depression can reach one's nerves. We can think dark thoughts during these times. Our thoughts can be very persuasive around these times, weakening the Heart even further. Many times it is the idea one will never be happy again that holds back the Heart from opening to the reality that happiness is its natural state. It is when the Mind's expectations interact with the expectations of the world that the trouble begins. One's expectations may be what is standing in the way. One's evaluations may be the missing piece of the puzzle to put it all together, to make one present. The Mind longs to be where it reasons is best to be, but one's 'best' is already defined by the longings of one's Heart. To deny the Heart is to deny oneself, whether by a reduction of one's Being or the neglect of one's truth. This can become a habitual problem and depression and loneliness commonly ensue from this point. A person may have limited their desires to some worldly source, or they may be unacquainted with the nature of the world's economy.

Because our Person longs to be, the Heart grows to covet and appreciate those places where a Person feels they can fully express themselves. This way, we grow connected to people, places, periods, and laboral purposes. We feel positively about them. A susceptibility of the Heart is its tendency to open up to the degree it feels it can be received. We can come to love these 'places'. This is perhaps the Heart's greatest susceptibility. The longings of Body and Mind dance with certain Spirits and places to create a special song with Desire and Purpose with and for them. It can make a home in them and the Heart loves and longs for the homes it builds in its lifetime. They become a part of it. These are the causes we invested our faith, hope, and love into. They are the items and ideas that have shaped our Hearts. They are the places we long to return to when the storm is strong, when all things pass, when the storm is settled. The places we love are home. They are like oases in this damned desert of a world. And while many confuse love for a feeling, those who love understand love know it to be independent of reason and feelings. They are beloved for a reason beyond reason. True love is present even when presence lacks. People do not decide who or what they love, Nature does. Much of the Heart is a product of flow, not intention. This is why lust is not love. Partnerships can be dissolved, conditions may be broken, bodies may age, but love remains.

Such unconditional appreciation is not found in infatuation, a condition frequently confused for love. Many in our time confuse love for infatuation. Infatuation and love can co-exist, but they are not the same. In fact, they are not even close. They just possess the individual in similar ways. Infatuation carries most of its weight through Mind and Body, it does not spring from the Heart. Like a virus, it actually infects it. Infatuation is borne out of complexes and disorders already present in the Mind. Complexes are results of one's historical relation with the world around them. In the case of the infatuated person, that individual uses the relationship with an object or person to achieve mental ease. The situation is comparable to that of addiction to a narcotic. In fact, it is one of its key features. The presence or absence of the object longed for largely determines the state of mind of the infatuated person. In love, this can happen. But nearly always, the condition of infatuation is predicated on what the infatuated person is receiving from the object in question. In the situations where one is not receiving anything from that person, place, or thing, it could be delusions from the Mind that are fueling the continuation of the obsession. This most often comes in the form of a 'hope' of some kind, a desired change wherein the object infatuated over finally begins to reciprocate some of the yearnings the infatuated person has been sending. Once again, the enamorment is contingent on what the Mind and Body expect to receive. Love does not mind such things.

What is loved is loved by the Heart and what the Heart loves centers us. It aligns the senses to the Mind, Body, and Spirit. It brings a practical sense to Desire, drawing our Heart back in line with the Nature it pays homage to. It steers us away from the psychotic tendencies of enamorment. Love puts us back on our feet. This way, our Hearts are like a compass. They guide us in the dark. When we are lost, they can lead us back. Our Heart has the power to bring us back home. When we are lost, we may simply be lacking orientation, but it never feels that simple when we are in this state. When we are far away from what we love, it feels very much like being far away from home. And just as compasses can break, our Hearts can lose the connection with Mind and Body to guide us. The order they are in place to provide may be compromised. We may grow confused. Anger can take over a perspective. And in the heat and harm of a conflict, love can leave us. Someone's heart can become so offended that it shuts us out. We reserve the right to do the same. It could be that we are no longer able to return to the places we call home. In some instances, the World rescinds the privilege to call it home at all. We can be ripped away from our homes. These are commonly very painful moments and from this we get one of the Heart's greatest susceptibilities, its susceptibility to be broken.

The Heart can break in a variety of ways, for a variety of reasons. Ultimately, heartbreak means the same thing. The Heart becomes unable to provide the lifeforce it works for. The ability to self-actualize is inhibited or even disabled. It is a deep wound to the identity, the functions of the psyche, and the neurological demands of our personalities. It is an injury that pervades into every part of the Person. It is characterized by a profound loss of personal and emotional orientation, commonly culminating in the existential challenge to identity. It produces great mental disorder. The ability to serve our value systems as we know them is severed. We may lose the ability to assess our values. Consequently, we are removed from what we love even when it is right in front of us. We may even lose the ability to love. Profound love can destroy a person because the bond between the Mind, Body, and Spirit can be structured to depend on the presence and response of a loved item. Heartbreak is essentially a severe impairment to our ability to harmonize Mind and Body, silencing out the Heart, resulting in the closing of one's Spirit. The Heart can mourn many things, including things it was once not grateful for or even aware it loved. To the degree one loves, one hurts.

For example, when one is physically injured, one mourns the loss of an ability. When one is psychically injured, one mourns an ability perceived to be lost. When one's soul is injured, one's existential purpose is threatened. All of these can open wounds deep enough to break a Heart. A wound is a wound for a wound is a wound in a wound. In either respect, the Mind's orientation, structured by the value system it has set up the distribution of attention and emotion, as well its accompanying goals are lost. Capacity is very much a mental orientation drawn out from one's self-esteem. A broken Heart greatly inhibits our ability to be efficient. A person may lose the incentive to bathe, eat, or remain sober. Their care for deadlines or work may subside, even disappear. Suicide is rare, but ideation is common and it is not as far away as we think. For the heartbroken, days bleed into one another as they lose their footing on the passage of time.

The heartbroken person misses the past, resents the present, and dreads the future. Life becomes akin to a war. The longing for what 'was' really stands to represent the peace and stability the Heart enjoyed before the 'war'. Under the light of fears coming true, one exists shaken and disturbed. The first heartbreak breaks the ability to trust unconditionally. One must cope with the newfound reality of what Life, Nature, God, or even their own hand has dealt them. One may not understand it is the nature of love itself to hurt this way, that it hurts because it matters. The way one hurts, what one misses, the pain one feels will all depend on the unique nature of each heart and the nature of the love needed. In a physical case, losing the ability to walk will ask one to accept all the things one didn't get to do with the ability to do so. In a psychic case, one may be forced to live without a special someone and be dealt the hand of learning to embrace themselves as an individual independent of the relationship. Or in the case of a profound bond like that of child and parent, we speak of the soul, a case where one may be forced to live without their Body's beloved. The Heart can be broken in a variety of ways, it only depends on the way one is loved and the dreams and hopes one had for that love. The consistent element among heartbreak is a tormentous resistance to embracing a set of circumstances once dreaded and feared.

In heartbreak, the Person perceives themselves to exist outside of the Light. One feels as though they are in the Dark. To the person existing outside of heartbreak, I would ask them to imagine existing without the pain of losing what they love most. Then, I would ask them to multiply this pain. Furthermore, I would ask them to live without this loved item. Some people get their hearts broken over and over and over again in a lifetime. Some people only experience it once. In either respect, the experience can lead us to grow bitter, vain, or materialistic. The inability to cope with heartbreak causes people to adopt delusional admirations of money and pleasure. They may distract themselves with consumption. This is all because of the refusal and fear of experiencing the recovery process and facing the truth of what it means for one's worldview. Heartbreak changes a person. They may refuse to dream again. The Mind can live empty and depressed. The Heart may not open up again. The Light dimmers and the ability to love fades. As love fades, so does the Person.

The Heart is not in the center of the chest as the physical heart is, it is in every part of our body. It is in each cell. So when someone is heartbroken, it will manifest as trauma, depression. A person will be physically impacted by it. Attempting to try new things will naturally provoke anxiety. People struggle to communicate this. Feet may not think but they can be rendered immobile. A scientific understanding will ask for a kind of process, but I believe there is worth in listening to the Person themselves. Poetry will be gutted by doctors and psychiatrists to filter out the few dribbles that could result in a diagnosis. The Mind should not be confused with the Heart. The Heart is nothing outside of Nature, it is the flow of Nature and one's relationship to it in each Person. When a Heart is broken, a Mind is depressed, a body loses its motivation. A Spirit loses its willpower. It could be the Mind loses control and the Body takes over. We can become slaves to the body as we try to find some comfort from our troubles. It is by virtue of a broken Heart that the body's neurotransmitters will pull the person down and away from what they know is good for them. The chemicals are then not the end, but the result. Those brain chemicals are more often the ends than the cause. Nothing of the Heart is supernatural in this respect. We just haven't realized its pertinence in our own self-understanding. We don't walk straight without it.

Recovery from Heartbreak demands tremendous commitment and consistent reiteration. This is particularly true if the process occurs alone. It is a spectacular thing to witness a Heart put itself back together. People do it every day. Yet, many do not understand. Not even those who do it understand it. Nowadays, medications are thrown at the brain before an investigation of the Heart is conducted. Love could be what is lacking, not a certain chemical compound. The mimicry of love's effects by the administration of these compounds is not love. Depression can kill people. I have seen it. The Mind is so powerful that some among the poor live with greater Heart than some among the rich. The body is so powerful in influencing the Mind one will not be able to see how their intolerance for work is really a fear of failure. A fear of intimacy can be an extension of the fear of rejection. One may be angry because of a knot in one's memories of the past. A broken heart must encounter and conquer all of these conditions. With the proper support, a Heart can and does overcome all of them. Most of us come to live broken hearted only with a period of time away from the injury. This is like calling a broken leg healed only because one can walk on it. Most people one encounters on a daily basis are on some point of the recovery process. The commitment to one's livelihood could have been what brought someone back on the assembly line, not a total recovery. What occurs with a broken Heart is a partial or total collapse of the ability to connect with the world around us. In an effort to preserve itself, the Mind enters a mode that rejects all stimuli that reminds us of an old hurt. The Body follows suit.

The Heart has to be understood in the sense of what it stands for. It stands for union, of self, with others, with the world, and our sense for the creator. The world today understands the Heart as a metaphor, a word for Self before Mind came to be understood. Remember what we said about words. We reduce our Hearts to an organ but to do so would be talking about an entirely different thing. There is water between and beneath each bridge keeping each person apart just as the oceans separate the continents. But like the continents, there is land under all the oceans. We are all connected underneath the surface of the water. Yet, we fail to see this when our waters are not clear. Each person's Heart is like an island in and of itself where rivers of love, pools of hate, and monuments of effort and time define it from the rest. Much like dolphins peer out from under, so do our thoughts. They come up to the surface to our conscious imagination. Every thought that comes out of the water is soaked with that water. So if a thought is ugly, coated with a mean tone, or with an image we do not like, they tell us of what is below. We may not be evil, our own unconscious waters may just be polluted, muddy, or dirty. From our thoughts come our words, from our words, our actions and this what keeps Hearts apart, just as oil and water keep apart. It is rarely the action that is remembered, but the feeling it caused.

Because of the susceptibilities of the Heart, one's actions are never as they seem. A person who has matured is able to recognize someone who is hateful, hurtful, or insecure. Someone who understands heartbreak understands the ugly extent we can go to in order to escape the throes and the pain. They know the hatred, the ugliness, the wrath that can come out of a person who is hurt. One reaches a point where they are about to spot the product of a blackened, closed, or weakened Heart. A closed Heart is like a closed bridge. It has rejected the external, deeming it poisonous, risky, or 'unworthy'. A hardened Heart does not trust and struggles with loving and being loved. Closed Hearts perhaps suffer the most. There are many of us who are there. In this darkness, it is imperative we wonder what is hurting each person and how that is translating to what that person is doing and what they are dedicating themselves to.

These understandings take a great deal of effort and humility. To the one who has suffered betrayal, to forgive or return to the transgressor may be stupidity, even if the Heart longs for such a peace. This is Mind preserving Body. If memory and emotion are involved, the emotion, if neurotic, can come to taint the Soul. We come to be ruled by the resentments of those transgressions we failed to get past. We may not recognize them, but they are present in the Mind's likes and dislikes. We are shaped by them. These likes and dislikes come to affect Personality to the extent they drape our Hearts with identities, aesthetics, and philosophies. All of this so that our Mind finds some comfort from the confusion, some stable ground. These likes and dislikes can lead us to appreciate vanity, admire arrogance, and glorify materialism. We can trap ourselves in industries, social circles, and institutions mired in sinful practices. They are distractions to the issues of the Heart and it is a susceptibility to avoid what we know we must do.

Ultimately, transcending and maturing from our vanities and our unreasonable likes and dislikes is key to resolving the troubles of the Heart. Incorporating what is worthwhile and avoiding what is not takes Heart. Transcending the pain begins with the arduous journey of becoming acquainted with it, enduring it, and embracing it. There is no good in running from it. Rejecting the pain only serves to reject oneself. It is not a pleasant life to be running from the contents of one's Heart. It is a wise life to understand which contents are worth running after. There is no necessity to live life as a war. There are only very few who achieve a peace after it.\ We do not have to make this any harder for ourselves. The Mind fights itself and the body follows suit with self-destruction. Care leaves. The possibility of forgiveness grows distant. War becomes likely. We cease to share. Consequently, we cannot love. We become hesitant to give, especially not of our Hearts. Relief will give one the internal room to see that the past is okay, that the present is necessary, and that the future will always remain fundamentally out of our hands.

Among all broken hearts lies a small gap where one

hopes the pain will end. This is where the path to transcend Heartbreak begins. It may go against every fiber of one's being to do so. It will ask to reassess one's old priorities, one's old conditions and find the strength to move past them. The Mind may be tied to a lover, the Heart may be tied to a duty. It perhaps failed them both. We are not evil because we fail. One may have been at war with something beyond them and had to do things that were necessary for that person at the time. Whatever it was, we did what we had to do. We must forgive ourselves for letting us get to those places we got ourselves into and accept the fact we were there and all the things we did there. There is no thought that comes to acceptance and incorporation without our own permission. We have to forgive ourselves for breaking our own Hearts. One moves past the susceptibilities of the Heart by becoming acquainted with how our Mind takes us away from ourselves. One moves the susceptibilities of the Heart by coming to respect the body, learning the mind, and never leaving one's soul in another's hands. One's Heart is fortified when it is in the natural harmony its God has made it for. Then, we are happy. Only the Mind can leave us obsessed with comfort, the delusion that in this world there is something better to give or receive than the Love we have to share. Upon finding this love, my friends, we can begin our journey in this life to find out Who God Could Be.

The Sculpture

Sweetness of my Heart,
Channel of my love.
The uniting force in me,
How sweet is thee.

I feel with thee,
In thee, I feel so small,
And me, the luckiest I can be,
feels graced to be in it at all.

So light of my light, fuel of my fiber,
in each thread of You I am,
And with each tear I cause,
You sow it together by virtue of your Divine Law.

With Your hand in mine,
I inherit your artistry.
I am gifted, not made,
And in my remaking, I am taken and given.

Fire of my fight, sage of my sight,
Keep this being intact while I battle
with your divine might.
Truly, in this, I endure the most lovely plight!

Into the night, I will go.
Apart from my beloved and devoid of comfort I know.
We wander into the jungle where we ought to grow.
What love will I come to know!?

In standing the cold and tending your holy farm,
Letting be what comes and letting go what harms,
I will remember what is wrong and I do intend to get to those
limits this being was meant to know all along.

V

Who God Could Be

What if I promised you that everything that occurs is in some form or fashion 'meant' to happen? What if every step we take, every word we say, and every thought we get is on the course of the longest and most elaborate story ever told. I might argue it is the only story that is really being told. I believe we are a part of that 'story'. I believe many, if not all, come to realize this, too. And if one lacks the capacity or the prior experience to sense ultraversal arrangement, you likely won't feel a thing as I put these words forth. They may sound mad or delusional. In that case, carry on. However, our detest for the cheap, our valuation for what 'helps', one's taste for More, and the urgency to grow are all signs you're a part of It. Your cells carry the knowledge already present in your Heart waiting to take you in the direction the Lord has predestined for us all since before we were born.

This life is not about the identities we hold. Yet, many confine it to that. It is not determined by our words, despite the fact we can elicit an effect from them. Existence as a whole cannot be perfected by our relationships. What good is it to reduce others to the descriptions we hold them to? Many listen to 'reason', but few listen to the Heart. People cry out for things to 'work', tormented by the delusion they aren't. But I propose that even in mistakes there is perfection, that even the cancer cell makes no mistake. We may never investigate the reality of a situation because we don't like the feeling thinking about it incurs. What would happen if someone simply stopped believing everything one thinks to be true? What if the life we have lived, the structures of social understanding that have dominated their course, what if for a moment they looked past them? What if life was imagined or even lived beyond the definitions? If one could separate one's work, life, self from the bullshit classifications, what then? What is left? Without your words, your names, your descriptions, who are you? Are you who you think yourself to be? Were you made? If you don't like the idea of a creator, what about being a part of the system that has gravity taking zero days off? Is anyone willing to trust that maybe we are going in a *perfect* direction, as intimidating as that may be? Yes, human existence is dripped in suffering, but we stress too much from a mere overvaluation of this sliver of existence.

We spend our days gossiping about the nature of other's intentions, about things outside of control. We speak of them as though we could control them. While our feelings and thoughts may guide our behavior, is it not the electricity in our nerves, the substance our bodies are made of, the subatomic arrangement innate to them that is running the show? Every occurrence after this whole thing started is followed by a reaction. With this in mind, wouldn't it make a bit of sense that

What if every argument, every separation, every meeting, every kiss, every wave or frequency our senses get to interact with are in a way 'destined' to happen, what then? Those things that burden your Heart, that make you writhe in your bed at night, burning your mouth and your gut, what if they were all in a sequence perfectly machining a very visible order? What if that order was Nature itself? It very apparently seems to be so, but what if Nature was being guided or structured by an even greater Nature, one that may have created or facilitated it? What if we were in motion with it as we live out our day to day? Because as far as we know, our little 'free will' is something only pertinent to our perspective. Nature, though generous in its donation of this perspective, does seem to be limited by our silly, confined will. Nature obeys a broader mission. Our substance is transforming and transposing itself according to a blossoming and patternized maturation process being constantly catalyzed by Nature. There is majesty in the fact of our existence, glory in its presence alone. Instead of realizing what we exist in, we choose to curse the parts that fail to produce in line with our desires.

  We may sense and feel then think and finally speak what we feel is our most fervent truth in the moment, releasing from the Heart what we felt we needed to. But no matter what we say, our word is not the Word. It's not everything, it is not Truth itself. Our words are just acoustic vibrations,but the Word is the funnel through which we were all made. By the Word, we get to be. This whole thing, the entirety of the Word, gets to Be in you. Amazing as that is, we don't run everything. Whatever is moving the universe, whatever compilation of forces propelling its infinite expansion, is present in us. It also precipitates all the movements and urges of the Heart. It is in our instinct, the reproduction of our cells. This way, while we may be going around doing what we 'feel' is right according to the world of idols, seeking to find relief from the susceptibilities of the Heart, our drives are not the organization of the Universe. They are a manifestation of the Universal Order in motion. You get to be a part of **it all**, your life is a part of it. Your Will is the channel through which Order works itself. You are not divorced from the greater Order, at all. It takes a humble heart, however, to realize one's place and to accept it without an inflation of the ego.

    The religious all have their claims about a maker, an organizer. Each has their own methodologies and vocabularies to hiss at the 'non-believers'. They scold and warn. Yet, by the same Substance they judge with, they are also driven to make the same mistakes as those non-believers. Guilt and personal insecurity often plague these kinds of religious. This is because many religious people too often obey words, they pray to the Rules. They evaluate their lives according to the quality of their obedience, to how tediously they maintain what they think is 'holy' or 'righteous'. But the organized religions too frequently see the representatives, the priests, the gurus come to reverence. Is this not another idol? Simply because one has read the works of the scholars, that is no indication they have grasped the Substance in their psyches or care for it. One may be oblivious to the God functioning in us, to our relationship with Existence as a whole. Those you revere and love perhaps have not, either. Maybe you cannot see that whatever is determining or directing your existence is electing you and everyone you know to play out its enormous function. The function of our existence is working inside, behind, above, and beyond your identity. This grand chemical organization does not take the orders of the priests. These orders have produced You as you are now. They made the priests priests. All of this makes a conversation seem like more than a conversation. It can make people seem like perfection. It makes everything like a flower blossoming before your eyes. This way, religion is not the end. It can be seen as a tool, a chapter in our history, that the Order nested in us to get us closer to realizing Its presence. The church is not God and we must not confine our beliefs to the claims they have for the nature of the Substance. We should get inspiration from what we can instead.

    Chaos, pain, and injustice is merely a result of an Order our egos have yet to understand. They are results of our inability or refusal to accept the nature of reality, of that Order, in our everyday life. We hope and pray. We suffer and in that, we may be tempted to condense this chaos to a sort of conditional freedom. We think that maybe if things went this way or life went that way that maybe things will be 'alright'. But the whole time, we may be blind to the fact that our hopes and dreams are the Order organizing every man's dreams and reservations into the place it deems fit. Despite all the probabilities around, it is all going to happen the way it was going to happen. Nature worked itself to produce a certain condition and its rules will not bend in our lives. Men who have realized this have made it into the history books. But far too often, we think more in the qualms of perfecting our obedience to society's taste than understanding and working what is driving our urgency to do that. The urgency to worship, to grow, to have fun, to eat, to sleep, to rest, to make love are all cumulative desires made possible by an unfathomably deep arrangement. We are barely beginning to understand it. Our chemical properties show themselves in our desires and our actions. Yet, vain are our commitments, arrogant are our attitudes, and blind are our Hearts. If with a shred of humility we could see the world, maybe we can see that whatever God is lies not in the lines we draw in the sand or how perfect we draw them, but in the arrangement, matter, and administration that led us to draw them in the first place.

    God would not be one thing, or one man, or a woman. A

'maker' of the universe' cannot be confined to an idea, much less a political ideology, or some symbol. We cannot condense God to a human purpose. The God of All would not be like an everyday man. The God of All would be closer to the infinite, sustaining, and conglomerated union of all of existence's features, their propellers, and more. He would be in every man. So the religious institutions served us, they did. They oversaw our political, social, and spiritual matters. But I argue the words they used, the duties they carried out daily were all part of what I like to call the Will of God, even the ugly parts. There is nothing that happens without the permission of the Lord. Our own minds and its arrogance trap us to lives based in the delusion that God is somehow limited. They trap us to live our lives determined on obeying, defending, and spreading our decrees without living them out. We believe God is something capable of being doubted. In our age, I see us try again and again trying to treat the All as something that could be reduced to such a thing, person, or idea. We kill for it. I believe we can find that God cannot and should not be reduced to a pawn of autocratic control, a tool to control. It need not be a metalaw. God need not be a methodology of analysis or a set of statistics or a collection of facts.

We do not have to reduce what is not reducible to fit what is not fittable. Until we realize this, we will keep fighting one another in the name of 'God'. The word 'God' itself is enough to draw cringe from many anti-religious. The atheists find their moral solace in the enforcement of laws. The relativists mold the moral narrative. Many rest in the ideas their lives are safe, right, and sound. But, we are not 'right' because of what we did nor 'wrong' because of what we have not done. Who God could be would not be limited by these measly definitions. Who God could be would not be something accessible to geniuses, scholars, or priests alone. If God could evaluate us, that God would have an intimate understanding down to the arrangement of each cell. We do need to be esoteric about this 'God'. For the name of God has been given many turns, and one of the closest markers we have is that God is what *is*, what has been, and what will be. That God is everywhere. Maybe who God could be is the What, as well.

Bringing God into our fingertips can delude us. The false ego can lead us astray to confuse the false ego with the Self beyond the personality. Perhaps this is the curse Adam and Eve faced, maybe it is what is driving the idolization and infatuations we suffer from today. We cannot assume the great arrogance that we are the entirety of the What. We are not every instance, every atom, and every moment. We have our place in it, but we are limited. Arrogance manifests in the possession of qualities or traits that do not belong to one. Who God could be would not be limited to creation alone. He would not be confined to our thoughts nor our works. What good would it do to convert the whole world to a certain religion? What good would it do to do such a thing, but fail to spread the love and respect the prophets heeded to us? What good would it do the scientist to understand all the matter in the world but not realize the God in action in its function, or in his or her actions? The hyper-religious end the conversation when it gets ambiguous. And the philosophers, even the greats, have remained limited by the cultural and semantic barriers of their times. To confine one's interest to the world is to miss out on the incredible amount of space between us and infinity. No intelligence can access the Reality of our Specialty without the humility of recognizing that God would not be a word, a religion, nor an idea.

Unfortunately, according to the logic I have presented, every commoner who has submitted to a religion is by our language 'wrong'. I see that by the vocabulary and definitions of the world, one may feel compelled to say so. However, in the language of expression relevant to the Universal Order, they were not. They absolutely were not. As long as they existed, lived, did, procreated, aged, and died, they did just fine. As long as anyone was, they did okay. In the way of Being, they were perfect. As ugly as that may seem, as ugly as some deeds were, as awful as some have made us feel, however treacherous and deceptive some actions were, they were all in the Story, too. Even in the moments one was done wrong or did wrong, I suggest the thought that even down to the impulse that catalyzed the action, it was serving its purpose in the Will of God. From the level of that human perspective, it likely felt like a choice. But in the grandiose and gargantuan mechanization that is Reality and beyond, that why will remain a mystery to us until we reach that beyond.

    Therefore, we must not grade lives. We mustn't confine the most complicated aspects of existence to a rubric of success conducive to this world of idols. We can be so quick to gauge someone's value by the ability we perceive of them. We can be very biased. We evaluate people under the light of the attraction we feel for them. We violate and undermine others' dignity when we take upon this sort of favoritism. We negate the ethical for the aesthetic. We negate and let go of what has worth and love for us for it, too. What a joke to live by the generalities and affinities of the crowd! Are we so lazy that we need to outsource our evaluations and determine our alliances by the feelings of another? In their arguments, is it not silly to confine our world to their worlds? Is that not equally as blasphemous as taking our thoughts blindly Instead, would it not be more fruitful for the Heart to see all creatures and every circumstance from the angle of God's lens? Maybe then we can ignore the colors society has painted onto the world and make some of our own. Not out of some duty, but some beauty one sensed emanating from creation. Can we humble ourselves for a moment and see for a moment that these 'wretched' creatures, too, are carrying out Nature's orders? Yes, even in their transgressions. Some were not privileged enough to know another way.

There is a place for all the bad we have done. Every disruption that warped in our understanding, all the events and 'lower' dispositions were all a part of Nature's process, too. We know how dark and inaccessible our Hearts can be. Imagine just how much hatred can be in a Heart. We know how estranged they can get from the Truth, from union, from love. Imagine being so foreign to love that even the hope of its acquisition is lost. Imagine one dedicated to hate because they have no belief that love has any worth. Or worse, the belief it will never return. Navigating the labels we ascribe the world, we can grow blind to what is and how it is in actuality. One rejects a heart of gold for a scar on the hand. It takes trust to open one's Heart. We have to humble ourselves unto another. And if we are inhibited by hate, we will not see that every cell in each body is on the course. They, too, received and lived under the accord we are a part of, regardless of what they did, spoke, and believed in their lifetime. I offer you that perhaps hell is in the spite we put on the name of the living and the dead. Even in the 'afterlife', our essence can be an experience to be suffered.

If we use our measly human terminology to project our judgements in order to divide matters into 'right' and 'wrong', we'll miss out on the fact that even a person who hurts and has hurt, failed, perhaps stutters, that leper, the known addict, even the poorest of the poor are facilitating that ever-rich Universal Order. Our feelings are, too. Even when you're intimidated or resentful towards someone, the feelings themselves are not the be-all and end-all of anything except the current position of our progress in life. They are simply an opportunity to realize it. For this reason, the only Christian who ever lived told us that if one slaps our cheek, offer them the next one. It is a gift for us both. In being shown harm, one can show the offender how impulsive and mindless they can be. There is no growth in teaching someone unwilling to learn. The reality of Who God could be can be lost in favor of Scripture's perfect recitation, in the sad disregard of its practicality in real time. With the understanding of oneness, it becomes something special to help your neighbor.

    The discussion about who God could be has been clouded by a judicial approach to the matter. We associate God too much with some moral lens, as though that it were ours to give out. When we speak of God, we do as though we were talking about a parent. Given the tone we take, our sentiments about God ring much like those of an adolescent. We are going around waving the wand of what is right and wrong. We have all these plans for the future. We seek out experiences, making an identity in spite of the patriarchal order of the old customs. We feel so strongly about our ideas. We talk of this or that as evil, trying to grow with the accelerated nature of our consciousness with its newest gadgets and technologies. We think we have it all figured out. But just because we have reached some tactile experience, some global institutions, some sense of identity, I don't think we have the right to be arrogant. I am one to frown on the idea that a man is judging our actions like a federal judge at the highest possible circuit. We need not be delusional or carnally incentivized in our conceptions of a divine regulation. We need not confine God to the rules and religions that rule us, nor His goodness to the pleasures and riches that elude us.

    We are looking for something. That is easy to see. Atheism is growing fast and many religious are tuning out. Many are turned off by what people feel is a hypocrisy in ecclesiastical or clerical matters. In the congregation, many will attend with their most esteemed apparel. And as they sit next to one another, many will make no effort to get to know the one next to them. Our interactions, sadly, get shadowed by some consideration of one's standing within a group. A believer in the All may not know how to do the sign of the cross, but a true Christian would not mind one bit. The congregation listens to the preacher speak of this dogma, or this prophet or that belief. Yet, I always asked what about the priest is more special than that quiet dreamer in the back pews? Or the sinner in the shadows? I think of the nun not allowed to be in his role and the fact that the nun bears the power to bring life? Does one really believe our God, giver of Life itself, would have a problem with life-bearers representing His Holy Arrangement? That somehow our relationship with the prophets is inhibited by the fact the preacher is not a man? Is that same man not limited by his education, which came from men, and preaching to men? I think the majority of sensible adults would agree if they go beyond their dogmas. That, however, is a risky avenue to take. Otherwise, the conversation starts steering in the direction of hellfire and punishment. They never went up to Jesus and asked him what it meant when he said that there was no right or wrong, only 'One'. Ironically, we long to feel 'whole'.

Are we so spiritually out-of-touch with ourselves as a species that we must rely on pompous, vain, arrogant men? Must our desires bleed into theirs? Must we succumb to careers, and venerate institutions to feel a wholesomeness that comes only from realizing oneself? While we must dedicate ourselves to a cause, can we say with certainty that we are consciously choosing our path? Do we have to remain in the vanities that lead to greater persuasions, covered by ever-more elaborate deceptions? Do we have to sell our bodies to others for the satisfaction that can only be sensed and gained from our self-esteem? Do we really leave it all behind for a neverland that holds a tiny comfort? Should we do that under the evidence of a much greater protection? Do we so quickly forget just how unlikely it was for us to be the way we are as we are? Given all the other ways things could have happened, we did.

Learning to love and appreciate formed the basis of my understanding of Who God could be. It started with an awareness of my existence, what that means, and what my actions have led to, what they meant to others. In a shell shocked despair, I came to know hope. What I took for granted became the one thing I wanted most. In my darkest hour, I learned how to cherish and crave the smallest victories. When in despair, smiles are like drops of water to a thirsty individual. In my loneliest loneliness, I learned how to love. I drew the patterns between the different 'schools' of thought I learned about. I observed and heard a million explanations from many men about this world for the world. Using sense, I aggregated the conversations, their contents, the causes and consequences of conflicts and saw how they overlapped one another. I saw them in myself and myself in them, reflecting on how I was treated and how I treated others. I went so far into myself, I came to meet parts of me I didn't know. I came to know myself when I had no one else to give me a hug.

Only in isolation did I ever come to these socially unacceptable tenets, these *ludicrous* ideas, such an appreciation for the genius, the beggar, the insane. Only in the Dark did I ever come around to the fact that you and I are perfectly imperfect, protected, and divinely loved. I came to imagine the prospect that death as we know it is only a change of scenery in this thing called existence. I came to appreciate the gift of getting to be who I was and being that person. I got to learn about myself as a Being and my relation to all Being. For a while, I came to be happy with the simple fact that I was alive. I only got to meet that after being so devastated, delusional, manic, apathetic, careless, pathetic and suffered. Despite all of that, I got to know the You in you, the You that makes me me, that makes us cousins with the trees. I got to meet my Self. I thanked God for the pain. Because every time I was scared to try, or speak, or go, or see, or be, I realized that all of my experiences were there with You. When I first got a sizable idea of who God could be, I had to relearn everything. The very contemplation of who God could be changed my life.

Because what do you do when you have sensed that everything that is happening is confined by a very limited perspective? That let-down is brought up by the fact that in our real Self, we exist in spans our Minds cannot fathom. One can begin to see oneself as a Thing within the All. What should one do when every symbol and memory and pleasure one has come across is nothing really but a history coming from It to you? What if Nature were to come in and burn down that little dictionary you hold on to so fervently for your 'sanity'? When what is happening to you is not limited at all by the internal or the external, one realizes one is the bridge between both. You see there is a duality only in perception. One learns to see past here and there, one can open the Other in the Mind. We can break the barrier between what we can identify and what we are sensing. We are That Something. And that if something made That Something, then that something is really Something, an incomprehensibly large Something.

If nothing was ever 'made' and it has just been, then It has always been. As existent beings, we are included in Existence. Our person reflects and longs for that continuity in our personality, our actions, and legacy. Now, we are talking about the Heart of the matter. I have always wanted to say that I wanted something. But after meeting my existence, I imagined for a beautiful second that our existence is united without limit to the great beyond. You don't even have to 'be' somewhere for Being to be there. A part of the greater You beyond the you we conceive to socially get by will always be there. Existence is there and sharing that relation with all things is not a delusion. We are existence in our varying forms as much as we simply 'exist'. Who God could be is the decider of the form we assume at any given moment. I may or may not be a part of God's body. I could perhaps be a thought in God's psyche, or an extension of God, a fetus in Its Being. I have heard it said that God is the only thing that can exist. I do not know much for sure. However, I do know that I did not plan Life, I had no say in the outcome of Life, except maybe mine. I cannot say this was entirely my bidding. Who God could be is the Planner or the Plan or both. God could be the Source everlasting, all that is. God, being God, would be in every dimension something can exist. God would be present in everything beside them and inside of them, even where they 'are not'. God would not be limited by time, space, words, or any understanding like that. I know I can do all things through God, but I do carry the understanding that nothing will occur without His permission. What an idea to imagine all of that alive in each person!

So I pity the men and women who think they know others, who judge by the religious standard, who divide men between 'good' and 'bad', but have never met You. Anyone who does not know You lives in fear and trembling, spending their days chasing the trap that leaves them soothing their senses. They do not realize there is nowhere they can go where they can escape themselves. Like an analogy, My God, there is no place we can be without You. Those who do not know You live bored, pressured, and confined. Their lives are led by deadlines. They know not the freedom you have already set in them. Chained to the pulls of the Heart and the Spirit are the godless, easily fooled by the eyes thought to make one see. The eye that does 'See' is the one that keeps us illuminated to our Spirit's longing, the one that constantly calls us to be free. Our circumstances, though, set us apart. They make us do what we said we never would. In shame, we can depart. In love, we can fool our Hearts. We constantly put off the effort that would free us, that long awaited 'start'. We can always count on the fact that we are a part of something beyond good and evil. We don't have to stop what we're doing, we just have to tweak how we do it and see why we're doing it the way we are. We are all 'good' and 'bad' in our own way. We are two sides of the same coin. We just land on different sides sometimes.

    The Good, beyond the world, is like the building, restorative aspect of existence. The Bad becomes its co-dependent destructive opposite. Our societies are so young they believe 'good' and 'bad' is related to what people say is so, or what they feel is so. They cannot see they are part of the Good and Bad at work. Their feelings are extensions of Goodness. They are the universal forces in us. With respects to our God, You are working towards a mission, a divine dance with Matter, one in which I am Your puppet, working the false 'me' to get to how You want to be. The perception that beholds You knows it is limited and finite. If it is to face You, it must see beyond the container yielding the false self, the ego identity must be relinquished for a moment. To see the greater Self, to integrate existence as one's reality, we must forgive anyone who has ever hurt our perceiving body. For anything with matter and substance is, by its very existence, dependent on the forces sustaining it to keep it in place. Our existence reflects righteousness. Connection is in our bodies, the survival of our bodies and their functions are like love in motion. What consolidates and concedes builds upon love, it breeds connection. I have heard it said that God is love. I always wondered what that meant. It could be that our God is what decides good and bad. Our God perhaps has modeled our behavior to facilitate His Will. We have to understand that, if this is the case, God is beyond us in this respect.

Our substance knows what it is made of, some may say it is knowledge itself. We never had to teach our cells how to grow, nor hunger to tell us what it means, nor our Hearts how to love. We carry this God-given knowledge in our Substance about how to go on. Just as children grow through play, the flow of our Substance instills desires that are meant to take us to that Neverland. Our dreams have their place, as do our hopes. Just as we teethed in infancy, loved in youth, labored through adulthood, all events were different places on the current meant to lead us back to the ocean they pertain to. And with this, many may get discouraged. Many may feel out of control, but I urge you to not worry, for Rumi noted it best when he wrote that we are not a drop in the ocean, we are the ocean in a drop.

If we activate the potential to see in different ways, we can change ourselves by simply closing our eyes. With this simple movement, we can reduce the effect of the impressions on our psyche we receive from the 'external'. With closed eyes, we see nothing but what is within. After all, it is the back of your eyelids. When we stop caring about how we look to others, cathartic and artistic modes of being get activated from that outlook. When we combine these both, we get to experiment with ourselves in a very intimate and real way. This way, when we pay attention to ourselves, we are caring for ourselves. In tending to our states of being, like any crop, we can cultivate great harvests. In their neglect, like any crop left alone without water, a withering takes place. By caring for others, we are caring for our greater self. When we see ourselves as a Being, with value to be derived from Being, we fertilize something in ourselves. Our empathetic sense grows tremendously. In God, when we do someone wrong, we do ourselves wrong. With attention and introspection, we pull the weeds out of our psychic garden.

Even if a new 'maturity' is brought to our attachments, it

remains what it is. Instead, it is far more fruitful to take to the external not with a dedication of its excess consumption, but a special and intrapersonal relationship with its creation and its furtherance. Not for the sake of conceptions of self or the advancement of some delusion, but out of the permanent recognition of what we are. What if we could advance life for the rarity that it is. What if we could love our enemy? What if we could forgive those we love? What if we can forgive God for not seeing our wishes through? There are much greater fruits here. There is no need to grow resentful. Why plant seed on barren ground? The harvest is not always fruitful when you don't know its outcome. We will be angry. That is okay. We will be sad. That is okay. We will be disappointed. That is okay, too. This will hurt, but that is because that is what this human life affords us. We hurt because we are a part of something greater that 'wanted' it to be so. We are here because of something greater for something greater. In order to Be what we are, we have to endure It because It is also Being Itself in us at the same time.

    We cannot exist in constant consideration thinking about this 'greater' Self all the time. We do have work to do. For the human psyche, its contents are clouded with the attachments of this lifetime and the desires its carnality produces in it. Man suffers uniquely for carrying the privileges it has. All of Being is set to suffer in its own way. Its placement in Nature will determine how much one suffers. But all Goodness is found in the endurance of the condition besetting the sufferer. It is a win to simply be. We have a place here in existence the exact way we are. Seeing the pain through is only a 'test', if we could call it that. We are an experiment or outcome of Nature. Our 'test' is like a test run where Life 'sees' its mission of functioning and keeping the pace of growing. Our senses serve as the taste buds of a universe that digests its contents painfully. The Substance, the Greater You, grows as the smaller you does. Each episode in our lives feeds into the larger collection of experience as a whole. Our psyche may just have an affinity for something in this life. Maybe that desire wa

Many of us don't want to let things go. Many of us prefer the dark corners of memory. We remained tethered to whatever source of light lit that darkened room. To remain constrained by the egocentric consciousness, never deconstructing who you think you are, never reaching an idea of what you are, is like a swimmer who has not ever gotten wet. It is a tragedy to see the wasted potential of what could have been a whole person. It is a tragedy for the Heart to not attempt to carry out one's dreams. Life will bring us to points where we will get the chance to find out just what we are made of. There is no point to living our lives in the shadows of our fears, in the fear of being caught in some 'wrong'. It is not necessary to keep secrets, or lie, or form some responsibility to quietly indulge in it. The reason we enjoy anything we do is because that object of enjoyment and the relation of the senses we have to it is us. It is a part of Us. The You inside you rejoices to simply Be, presenting the Mind with the task of embracing the Body's present condition. This acceptance is where we can accrue love, it is not an easy thing to do. This way, love can be elusive from our persons because one continues to backslide in the ways of the Heart.

We may not realize who God could be is something beyond the words we use to describe It. When we ask for God, the You in you is asking to sense the stability and totality of presence. We get lonely and feel empty when we don't feel the presence of ourselves. Without the Self, we have nothing to communicate to God. We are the vessel that communicates the will of God guiding, sustaining, and harmonizing our Substance. With the appeal of luxury, our great delusions, and our inevitable confusion, we assemble our actions as though they were a ladder to You. We become senseless in the nonsense.

With broken hearts, we cry out to thee. Whenever I have cried out to You, the You in me was there to meet me at every molecule of every tear I have ever shed. I had to suffer loss to know what it was that gave me those gains in the first place. I learned there was never a time I was alone, despite all the times I felt alone.

No Man is alone with the Truth of what that Man is. It is not something that can be unlearned and it appears some people inherently know this. Anyone who has tried to transcend their pain knows this. The pains of our Hearts and the scars we bear shine forth as they foundations for self-reliance and our relationship with the Divine. We possess Truth in our Being. It has been said that God is Truth but I have also heard it said that He is the spring of everlasting life. As long as things are, everything is okay. A man named Jesus saw it that way. Once you drown in the waters of the Truth, you realize you were part of It all along. One sees one could never be abandoned, that everything is a blessing in its own form. The you that lived without seeing these blessings, constrained by the infantile ego ego consciousness, gets crushed by the weight of the reality it is under. It is not that one refuses to change, it is that person has been forcibly changed. The persuasions and deceptions that led that egocentric lifestyle often lose their weight, too. One's word comes to form a relationship with the Word. The deception loses its sweetness because the prize is no longer worth the cost.

One can get lost in One's search for God. It can be a long road back to your internal home, to the truths that make you feel like you belong. If you are lucky, you will find your way back even after that. There will be highs and lows that go on as long as months, even years. They can go every other way. We are all a part of something bigger, actively. Your life is comparable to the waves of the ocean, and all of its episodes dictated by currents led by winds that began incredibly far away. We have the power to make a heaven here in this lifetime through the efforts to fight our inner demons. The price of choosing the limited identity without realizing the infinite soul equates to the loss of the soul. I urge against permitting the fear of the Dark from the Light hidden within. One can get lost within it. Some spend their lives chasing crumbs on the floors of the dim-lit rooms of the Heart. With the Light, one finds it is never too late to share it with others. It may just be the only light they get in the blizzard of rejection. When we are lost, we have lost contact with the nature of ourselves. Getting in touch with this, developing an identity and changing it up, living up to our potential, is a large part of the experience of adulthood.

Death will happen, too. When disillusioned with an old order, a great promiscuity for chaos incrues. We begin to experiment, seeking out the new in what was previously deemed cheap or useless. The Heart seeks a new place to rest. A dying order is seen in the movements of the Heart, monumentally reflected in the acts in the ways one said they never would. The movements are the seeking Heart looking for an order to restore the power vacuum the old framework left behind. It is simply seeking its new order. These are the periods we are destined to endure in this life. They are waiting to happen to you. They're just not here yet. You are the laws of all Nature happening at once. You don't have to get 'out' or go 'in' and see. You are already seeing. *Meet the seer.*

The 'one' we cry and wait on is really the You in us crying out to be One. Our urges are directed to the tiny victories of the world, but really stand to reflect the manifestation of our Substance excited and ambitious to grow through every cell that encapsulates our person. It is as if the God within is happy when we succeed. The infant in us has not forgotten the stillness of the womb. And that long-lost stillness is sought after in adulthood in our longings to be 'successful', loved, 'whole'. We will always crave our first home away from Home.

All the while, our personalities endure and suffer. We carry on enjoying and sensing a world on our way to find the One meant for us. That One is the You beyond the definitions we have made for our Reality, far beyond any mental imagery. The eternally vibrant God that knows You as its child seeks to unite with your consciousness in this mission to see your life through. Life is simple this way. You just have to realize what you are and enjoy this life to the extent we can. We ought to find out who we can be, and do what that image demands of us. We do not need to go about it alone. We have God present. It has already had the whole thing planned out for You. It will happen the way It feels it needs to. You may not know what to do now, but you will when the moment comes. No worries necessary. It's got us, It always has, from womb to tomb and beyond.

We may not feel God's love. Given the nature of love, where union is not, love isn't either. Where division is, hate and fear rush into the vacuum of that space to take its place. The rules of chemistry come to affect our likings just as chemical dispositions determine the behavior of all elements. Life will have its way with us and that can affect our relationship with God and ourselves. See this, my friends. We may become blind by the veil our pains drape on our perceptions, the illusions they inspire. The prospect of Who God Could Be was what changed me. Surpassing my vanities, I came to love all that stands as a product of God, as though God is there. I figured God would be present even in his creation. The pains of this life make it hard to believe God is even here or anywhere. Division can make us feel all alone. But my idea of who God could be sees that God is in all that is and our life goes only in the accord God intends. The laws of Nature reflect that. In the reality of all this, I find refuge from the impressions that come. In my God, I find refuge. I am with You and You are with me. And now that you have read and entered my Heart, I feel that I am in a way with you. Because even if I am just a thought, or my words just a memory, they are different threads on the same article of clothing. We exist on the same fabric. In the knowledge of our protection, we can find this peace in who we are, as we are, when and where we are It. We find the capacity to accept ourselves, to accept our Hearts.

Ode to the Essence

You who have me,
who gave me my perception, from which I have gained
everything this body gets to perceive, You say hello through
Me.

This body seeks its reproduction,
with its vision clouding and shadowing the perfect union of all
things associated with it.

On this border between what one views to be oneself and the
world 'exterior'. I sense this will to exist, this urge to grow, this
commitment to stay, that I find present in me and all things.

This will is merely limited to the bounds and limits of Being
designated to that carnal object.

For while this Being cannot meet, love, and fall in love with a
rock and create Being there, one can at least, with physics'
permission, move that rock to a place where it will remain.

For the rock and myself, this will be enough for it and me to Be
and continue Being.

For something like life, like a cat, this Being is not as simple as
the loveless rock.

One has to look toward where the cat begins.

*This means one must take the most microscopic view
to find where the cat 'begins' and 'ends'. The beauty is in the
anatomical characteristics, the molecules in union, where the
costume of flesh tells where the cat 'begins'.*

*But really, one who can see the One knows there is no use to
see something that has no end and the end of something that
has no start.*

*Our Being, then, is sustained in a cell. But this being must then
go deep if it seeks to be understood In this light, likely
incomprehensibly deep.*

Still, Being sustains and maintains.

*This is because it wills to be. This requires no contemplation.
The natural law has already ingrained the code.*

But as we know, the Will is not all of Being.

*One's will has never been one's totality of being, it's merely one
facet of it for one to experience the One.*

*Foolish it would be, egregious the cost at my expense to
attribute my relative concepts, my measly sentiments, my
culturally defecated definitions, my most pathetically
ineffective vocalizations to try to confine thee.*

*For it is minutely perceived currently in the sciences just how
Being functions...
...and may it be that our humanity advances our
understanding to see the totality of It.
That is if God wills it.*

Our human eye has been allowed to absorb a portion of Being in this partial and finite perception.

This eye, enveloped and distinguished with ego, animated with speciality through body, guided Heart, finds itself acting to sustain and maintain itself.

<u>If we are, it is because we have been</u> sustained and maintained, because I know any measly act of my feeding myself that I may call an act of sustenance, is nothing in comparison to the gargantuan hospitality of our Universe's landlord.

Behold, my Love, Your canvas.
My case in point, I am drenched in Your paint.
I see only the colors You gave me, I wear Thee.
I am the evidence and testimony of our impossible and shared Being...
Just you and me.

Fleeting Meditations

The greatest fallacy of this generation is the belief Mind and Heart are the same thing.

Leave what you can, do what you must, see what you wish, but don't fail what you are.

What you like and dislike tell more of where you are in your development than the quality of the subject in question.

Some thoughts that never see the light of day illuminate the darkest parts of us that are stranded in the Night.

Never assume a thought you have to be yours.

Don't follow the lead of a thought without conscious consideration of its significances.

Someone's custom is someone else's wish.

Every instance of inaction is ingrained into reality after the fact.

The pursuit of happiness is often an investment with a fractional return.

Each day is a new life.

Chances are rarely earned so I deduce they could be given.

The separation, on the God question, amongst men begins at the question of whether the source of existence lies on a material or immaterial plane.

To seek and find is as common to Man as hunger and feast.

To waste means to not use for the permanent.

Being comfortable is not a sign of prosperity.

No action invalidates one, but one action can invalidate all.

Knowing when to see, when to hear, and when to speak are all separate skills with separate rewards.

Democracy only works if there is a habitual trust and honesty in a society's character.

Many religious hold and reserve Tradition as their god.

Everything a person says is what they would expect to hear in the situation they are speaking about.

Coming to a conclusion is not the end of a context.

Dining heavily frequently will make you look fat.

Restricting pleasure multiplies it at a later time.

The way language is obeyed in the tongue is the way Order should be obeyed in the Will.

Excuses are often your Will's consolations for it having betrayed you.

Reaching new heights sets you up for falling to greater depths.

Feeling good is not the same as being good.

Everyone has a general idea of what is right and wrong.

Right and wrong cannot be relativized but it is not black and white.

The Heart knows what the Mind knows not.

The Will is where God plays.

You cannot escape your duty without paying the price.

You cannot reason away the unreasonable.

Making a habit of needing sight to confirm reality will leave you short-sighted.

Power is more often found in indifference than difference.

Know when to risk, know when to be cautious.

Never believing you are done learning preserves the fertility of your spirit.

Every lesson is like a seed, watering it comes through the practice of practice.

Jesus was a smart guy.

The greatest people in history were just as human as you and me.

Loving your neighbor is a strange idea until you get the chance to.

The pursuit of an ideal degrades one's relationship with God.

You'll miss things running that you'd catch walking.

Many people have stepped over the land you are on currently.

With each person you meet, an echelon of history, intimacy, and Personality comes with them.

Fate and Circumstance in a way 'choose' to present everything they do to you in a moment.

Your responsibility is the Universe's asking of your part.

You incur debt when you put off responsibility, one way or another.

The administration of recreational drugs nearly always creates disorder in a person's life.

Being able and Being are different ideas.

If you can, do.

Put yourself in someone's shoes and you'll see why they did as they did.

It is incredible what one voice, one brain, and one heart have done to this planet.

The 21st century is one of a thousand cult of personalities promoted through greed and trivial nonsense.

Never confuse what a human does for what a human wants.

The true poet can read a book in a sentence by simply painting an image.

It is usually not the look of the eye, but *in* the eye that makes the difference.

I am not sure if people realize they never stop being wrong to a significant degree.

Relief is one of the most common goals actions try to satisfy.

Individuation completed through a quasi-conscious deliberation is shadowed and typically overridden by an equally complex unconscious opposite.

Learning the role of satisfaction serves exceptionally to identify the root of both short term and long term problems and plans.

Work, by human definitions, is the expense of energy for a specific outcome.

Rats don't like weed but they will die trying to get a coke bump.

It's downright miraculous how I can move my fingers today.

I could move my fingers yesterday too. What are the odds?

In this world, it is expected to play a character and being authentic is often looked down upon.

I always felt the best place on earth to make the idea of God concrete was the ocean.

I'm afraid of the ocean.

It seems like emotions are these little fractional versions of us that all battle to get their unique satisfaction through what we do.

You can tell who loved who more by the look in their eyes.

Everything is strangely connected and it's good to never forget that.

You do more harm in what you do not know and continue not knowing than good in what you do know.

The person you could be is hidden in some job position or career you negated, in a household where you aren't resentful, in a cause that betters the world you inhabit that you aren't attending to.

I think a large portion of life is waiting to happen to us and not the other way around.

The beauty of the Capitalist system I live under is that I can outsource meaning to money and material pursuit.

Belief kills the believer.

We get what we deserve, not what we want.

Plans evaporate when meeting practicality.

What we want is not what we deserve.

Hell resembles a place where you are in both excess protection and harm.

What you associate yourself with, you will gain.

Anger is brought about by the significance of things and events, not the things and events themselves.

Learning how you could be manipulated is a precept to shrewdness.

Those who are most dominated by their gods tend to be those who claim to not "have" any.

Trust is crucial to the progression of humanity as it brings about the harmonization of society.

I can prove the worthiness of trust by what can be and what is not.

How society feels about something you do can give you valuable information about that action and society.

Music opens the door to a transcendental state of consciousness.

Ask who God is, and I will ask what you spend most of your time on in a day.

I felt happiest in that chaos.

It is not my duty to do and fail, but it is to correct my failures.

Experience is not something that solely happens to you and everyone has their own interpretation of the same event.

Some thoughts are worth skipping.

One who did good but never had the choice to was a slave.

I plead with thee that I lose not my fire, lest ye put it out.

A lot of quotes come from phony intellectuals trying to sound smart to strangers.

An appreciation of history must begin with an appreciation of time.

You owe people for things they could have done but did not do that you would not have appreciated.

Violence is unfair.

Tomorrow is a place to be found later that is shaped by what you do today.

The tyrant distorts the truth to conceal his deception.

Most problems of communication would disappear if people were responsible and timely.

He who has seen and felt has absorbed knowledge cavernously.

You can find similarities in the function of a car to the function of a human adult.

A lot of life occurs in formulaic and structured response processes.

The laws of physics have a way in the laws of life.

Physics itself is not a predetermination, it is merely a measurable quantification of an empirically patternized phenomena.

Providing is one of the more noble forms of projection.

Everything has an element of something else to a certain degree and our biological tools found in body and mind are in place to determine those certain degrees of elements in everything.

Externalities purvey wisdom to all things human.

Pleasures fool the idealist and the idealist pleasures the fool.

Politics require philosophy in order to be ethical.

Degradation, in one's affairs, one's value, and one's family should be one's primary concern.

Equality of outcome is as dangerous as inequality of opportunity.

Shooting a blank round elicits the same response as a live one.

Humans in a mob resemble computers connected to the same algorithm.

Desire is a fire.

Calling to truth is the practical equivalent of praying.

Guilt is a vocable shadow creature living in the shadows of one's moral shelter.

Blame knows no limits and scapegoating has caused murder by the millions.

People have shot infants and beheaded children because of their beliefs before and during our lifetimes.

After our lifetimes, too.

What is true for individual tendencies tends to be true for collective ones, as well.

People should be more afraid of themselves than others.

The best deceivers tend to leave you feeling the nicest.

Pressure transforms the brittle, weak, and tired into the flexible, strong, and resilient.

Pain either brings out your best or makes you forget it.

One's opinion about governmental social services can grant you a rich insight into one's past and perspective.

A great way to create small talk is to point out an evident burden in a casual and non-accusatory fashion.

More friends are lost to romances than are to death.

How strange is it of the human to be aware of what needs to change but not have the will to change it.

A product can be a cause, motive, and consequence at the same time.

To find yourself being unable to distinguish the comfortable from the uncomfortable is the goal of discipline.

The glory of war is outmatched by its carnage. Every time.

It is always surprising how little we hold when it is all said and done.

Just because you are losing doesn't mean you have lost.

This could be the lowest you ever allow yourself to get....

One can become what they envision themselves to be only if they obey what that vision demands of them.

Tears shed in isolation and silence are priceless.

The most beautiful sunsets, I thought, always happened on my worst days.

I found myself in the passion of those figures and mannerisms of which I lusted for and passed into the night restless and unsatisfied.

Accept the equal limitations and mortality of another person and the anxiety they provoke in you will pass.

Sense authenticity and follow it, but don't let it fool you.

There are so many atrocities occurring at this very moment and yet the sky does not lose its charming hint of blue.

You will never find what you are looking forward to because it was in your hands and by your side the whole time.

The cycle has its roots in the circle.

Writing is testimony to human consciousness.

You can learn a thing or two from someone's opinion toward cats and dogs.

Imagining historical figures will make you smile.

You reveal yourself more in what you tolerate and laugh at than what you say and do.

Criticism should correct, not condemn.

We lack the right to go down certain avenues of thought.

Love can liberate or enslave.

The most common of tools were one once revolutions of their times.

The tragedy of genius is a society's tardiness in understanding him.

The genius dies under the weight of the ideas he carries.

I hope I never forget the person I was in this moment.

It is miraculous that I am exactly who I am, when and where I am it.

The reason life is hard is because it is a succession of goodbyes, one after the next, constantly.

Listen to what your body asks of you and consider why it asks this.

Plan so you can look forward to, act so that you can look back on.

In the end, getting what you want isn't all it is cracked up to be.

Refraining from following is the beginning of leading.

Leading something bad is not as beneficial as following something good.

All manifestations of Spirit get eroded into an ethical code over time that tries to replicate its momentary glory and we call this religion.

Division and pain are the remains of glory.

To fool into sympathy is one way, to fool into arrogance is another.

Humility is a way of life.

What if Jesus spoke from the perspective of God, like an actor, with the knowledge that he is God's child?

When not allowed to love openly, love secretly.

The psychological validation provided by social media is an expedient and cheap one that creates distortions and delusions about one's self-esteem.

They'll gaze and wonder how it could have been done and then turn around and do it themselves.

Knowledge met with the proper understanding alters you divinely.

And on that afternoon when I saw the clouds dance, I saw myself as I was, not who I thought myself to be and it was the most glorious.

Stop for a moment and watch that thought float across your mind like a shooting star in the night sky.

They cheat because they want the privileges of commitment without the price of it.

We speak ill of others to appear healthy.

We become crazy momentarily when we call something crazy.

Someone who stands with You can never be brought down except by You.

Your Heart knows, it always does.

Don't miss anything, bless everything.

On the other side of all of this, we will be there and you and I are going to have a great time in the place where there is no time.

Made in the USA
Coppell, TX
12 March 2025